AUSTRIAN COOKBOOK

Traditional Recipes from Austria

LIAM LUXE

Copyright © 2023 Liam Luxe

All rights reserved.

INTRODUCTION

This cookbook is like a map that will guide you to some of the best Austrian recipes. You'll find out how to make tasty dishes that people in Austria have been enjoying for a long time.

Austrian food is special because it's a mix of different flavors from Europe. Imagine the yummy taste of hearty meals, comforting desserts, and lots of history all rolled into one. That's Austrian cuisine for you!

In this cookbook, you'll learn how to cook some classic Austrian dishes step by step. You'll learn how to make things like Wiener Schnitzel, Käsespätzle, and even Sachertorte, which is a famous Austrian cake. Don't worry if you're not a pro in the kitchen; the recipes are designed to be easy to follow.

CONTENTS

APPETIZERS AND SNACKS 1
    Wiener Schnitzel Bites 1
    Käsespätzle (Cheese Spaetzle) 2
    Erdäpfelsalat (Potato Salad) 3
    Kartoffelpuffer (Potato Pancakes) 4
    Gulaschsuppe (Goulash Soup) 5
    Brettljause (Cold Cuts Platter) 7
    Obatzda (Bavarian Cheese Spread) 8
    Pilzrahmsuppe (Creamy Mushroom Soup) 9

SOUPS AND STEWS 11
    Frittatensuppe (Pancake Soup) 11
    Leberknödelsuppe (Liver Dumpling Soup) 12
    Kürbiscremesuppe (Pumpkin Cream Soup) 13
    Rindsgulasch (Beef Goulash) 15
    Kartoffelsuppe (Potato Soup) 16
    Gemüsesuppe (Vegetable Soup) 17
    Hühnersuppe (Chicken Soup) 18
    Linsensuppe (Lentil Soup) 19

MAIN COURSES: MEAT 21
    Wiener Schnitzel 21
    Schweinsbraten (Roast Pork) 22
    Tafelspitz (Boiled Beef) 23
    Hühnerfrikassee (Chicken Fricassee) 24
    Kasnocken (Austrian Dumplings with Cheese) 26

Rindsrouladen (Beef Roulades) 27

Rahmschnitzel (Creamy Pork Schnitzel) 29

Faschierter Braten (Austrian Meatloaf) 30

Hirschbraten (Venison Roast) 32

Gefüllte Paprika (Stuffed Peppers) 33

MAIN COURSES: SEAFOOD AND VEGETARIAN 36

Forelle Müllerin (Trout with Brown Butter) 36

Lachs in Dillsoße (Salmon in Dill Sauce) 37

Kartoffelstrudel (Potato Strudel) 38

Gemüsestrudel (Vegetable Strudel) 40

Kürbisrisotto (Pumpkin Risotto) 41

Schwammerlragout (Mushroom Ragout) 42

Potato Dumplings with Mushroom Sauce 44

Kartoffel-Gemüse Gratin (Potato and Vegetable Gratin) 45

Käsespätzle (Cheese Spaetzle) 46

Krautfleckerl (Cabbage Pasta) 48

SIDE DISHES AND SALADS 50

Erdäpfelsalat (Potato Salad) 50

Krautsalat (Coleslaw) 51

Gurkensalat (Cucumber Salad) 52

Rösti (Swiss Potato Pancakes) 53

Semmelknödel (Bread Dumplings) 54

Rote Rüben Salat (Beetroot Salad) 55

Kartoffelgratin (Potato Gratin) 56

Rahmspinat (Creamed Spinach) 57

Karottensalat (Carrot Salad) 58

Kartoffelsalat (Warm Potato Salad) 59

DESSERTS AND PASTRIES 61

Sachertorte 61

Apfelstrudel (Apple Strudel) 63

Linzer Torte 64

Topfenstrudel (Quark Strudel) 66

Esterházy Torte 67

Kaiserschmarrn 69

Palatschinken (Austrian Pancakes) 70

Mohr im Hemd (Chocolate Pudding) 71

Marillenknödel (Apricot Dumplings) 73

Mohnnudeln (Poppy Seed Noodles) 74

BREADS AND BAKING 76

Bauernbrot (Austrian Farm Bread) 76

Kornspitz (Seed Rolls) 78

Semmeln (Vienna Rolls) 79

Gugelhupf (Bundt Cake) 81

Buchteln (Sweet Rolls) 82

Austrian Pretzels 84

Lebkuchen (Gingerbread Cookies) 85

Vanillekipferl (Vanilla Crescent Cookies) 87

Marmor-Gugelhupf (Marble Cake) 88

Bienenstich (Bee Sting Cake) 90

PRESERVES AND CONDIMENTS 92

Hausgemachte Senf (Homemade Mustard) 92

Marillenmarmelade (Apricot Jam) 93

Eingelegte Gurken (Pickled Cucumbers) 94

Kren (Horseradish Sauce) 96

Apfelkompott (Apple Compote) 97

Rote Rüben Kren (Beetroot Horseradish) 98

Preiselbeeren (Cranberry Sauce) 99

Tomatenketchup (Tomato Ketchup) 100

Hollersirup (Elderflower Syrup) 101

APPETIZERS AND SNACKS

Wiener Schnitzel Bites

Servings: 4
Preparation Time: 20 minutes
Ingredients:
- 4 boneless, skinless chicken breasts
- Salt and pepper, to taste
- 1 cup all-purpose flour
- 2 large eggs
- 1 cup breadcrumbs
- Vegetable oil, for frying
- Lemon wedges, for garnish
- Fresh parsley, chopped, for garnish

Instructions:
1. **Prepare the Chicken:**
- Place the chicken breasts between sheets of plastic wrap or parchment paper.
- Use a meat mallet or rolling pin to gently pound the chicken to an even thickness of about 1/4 inch.
- Season the chicken on both sides with salt and pepper.
2. **Set Up Breading Stations:**
- In one shallow dish, place the all-purpose flour.
- In another dish, beat the eggs.
- In a third dish, spread out the breadcrumbs.

3. **Coat the Chicken:**
- Take a chicken breast and coat it in the flour, shaking off any excess.
- Dip it into the beaten eggs, making sure it's well-coated.
- Finally, coat it with breadcrumbs, pressing gently to adhere.
4. **Fry the Schnitzel:**
- In a large skillet, heat about 1/2 inch of vegetable oil over medium-high heat.
- Carefully add the breaded chicken breasts to the hot oil and fry until they are golden brown and crispy on both sides, about 3-4 minutes per side.
- Remove the schnitzel bites and place them on a paper towel-lined plate to drain any excess oil.
5. **Serve and Garnish:**
- Serve the Wiener Schnitzel Bites hot with lemon wedges and a sprinkle of fresh chopped parsley.
- They are delicious on their own or with a dipping sauce of your choice, such as tartar sauce or lingonberry jam.

Käsespätzle (Cheese Spaetzle)

Servings: 4-6
Preparation Time: 30 minutes
Ingredients:
For the Spaetzle:
- 2 cups all-purpose flour
- 3 large eggs
- 1/2 cup milk
- 1/2 teaspoon salt
- 1/4 teaspoon freshly grated nutmeg (optional)

For the Cheese Sauce:
- 2 cups grated Emmental cheese (or Swiss cheese)
- 1 cup grated Gruyère cheese (or another mild Swiss cheese)
- 1/2 cup grated Parmesan cheese
- 1 cup heavy cream
- 2 tablespoons unsalted butter
- Salt and black pepper, to taste

For Topping:
- 2 onions, thinly sliced
- 2 tablespoons butter

- Chopped fresh chives, for garnish (optional)

Instructions:

Prepare the Spaetzle:
1. In a large mixing bowl, combine the flour, eggs, milk, salt, and nutmeg (if using). Stir until you have a thick, smooth batter.
2. Bring a large pot of salted water to a boil.
3. To make the spaetzle, you can use a spaetzle maker or a colander with large holes. Hold the spaetzle maker or colander over the boiling water and pour some of the batter into it. Using a spatula or the back of a spoon, push the batter through the holes into the boiling water. The spaetzle will cook quickly and rise to the surface when done, usually within 2-3 minutes. Remove them with a slotted spoon and place them in a colander to drain. Repeat until all the batter is used.

Prepare the Cheese Sauce:
4. In a saucepan, melt the 2 tablespoons of butter over medium heat. Add the sliced onions and sauté until they are soft and golden brown, about 10 minutes. Set them aside.
5. In a separate saucepan, heat the heavy cream over low heat. Add the grated Emmental, Gruyère, and Parmesan cheeses. Stir until the cheeses melt and the sauce becomes smooth. Season with salt and black pepper to taste.

Combine and Serve:
6. Preheat your oven's broiler.
7. In a large ovenproof dish, layer half of the cooked spaetzle, followed by half of the caramelized onions and half of the cheese sauce. Repeat the layers.
8. Place the dish under the broiler for 2-3 minutes or until the top is golden and bubbling.
9. Garnish with chopped fresh chives if desired.

Erdäpfelsalat (Potato Salad)

Servings: 4-6
Preparation Time: 30 minutes
Ingredients:
For the Potato Salad:
- 2 pounds (about 4-5 medium) waxy potatoes (e.g., Yukon Gold or red potatoes)
- 1 small red onion, finely chopped

- 3-4 pickles (dill or sweet), finely chopped
- 2 tablespoons fresh chives, finely chopped
- Salt and black pepper, to taste

For the Dressing:
- 1/2 cup vegetable or sunflower oil
- 1/4 cup white wine vinegar
- 1 teaspoon Dijon mustard
- 1 teaspoon granulated sugar
- 1/2 teaspoon salt
- 1/4 teaspoon black pepper

Instructions:

Cook and Prepare the Potatoes:
1. Wash the potatoes and place them in a large pot. Cover them with cold water and add a pinch of salt.
2. Bring the water to a boil, then reduce the heat to medium-low and simmer the potatoes until they are tender but still firm, about 15-20 minutes. You can test their doneness by inserting a knife into one; it should go in easily.
3. Drain the potatoes and let them cool until you can handle them. Peel them (if desired) and cut them into bite-sized cubes.

Make the Dressing:
4. In a small bowl, whisk together the vegetable or sunflower oil, white wine vinegar, Dijon mustard, sugar, salt, and black pepper until well combined. Set aside.

Assemble the Potato Salad:
5. In a large mixing bowl, combine the chopped potatoes, finely chopped red onion, pickles, and fresh chives.
6. Pour the dressing over the potato mixture. Gently toss everything together until the potatoes are evenly coated with the dressing. Taste and adjust the seasoning with additional salt and black pepper, if needed.
7. Cover the bowl with plastic wrap and refrigerate the potato salad for at least 1 hour to allow the flavors to meld together.

Kartoffelpuffer (Potato Pancakes)

Servings: 4-6 (Makes approximately 12 potato pancakes)
Preparation Time: 30 minutes
Ingredients:
- 4 large russet potatoes, peeled and grated

- 1 small onion, finely grated
- 2 large eggs
- 3 tablespoons all-purpose flour
- 1 teaspoon salt
- 1/2 teaspoon black pepper
- Vegetable oil, for frying
- Sour cream or applesauce, for serving (optional)

Instructions:

Prepare the Potato Mixture:

1. After grating the potatoes, place them in a clean kitchen towel or cheesecloth. Squeeze out as much liquid as possible from the grated potatoes over the sink. This will help make your Kartoffelpuffer crispy.
2. In a large mixing bowl, combine the grated potatoes, finely grated onion, eggs, all-purpose flour, salt, and black pepper. Mix everything together until well combined.

Fry the Potato Pancakes:

3. In a large skillet, heat about 1/4 inch of vegetable oil over medium-high heat until it's hot but not smoking.
4. Take a heaping tablespoon of the potato mixture and carefully place it into the hot oil. Flatten it slightly with a spatula to form a pancake shape. You should be able to fry about 3-4 pancakes at a time, depending on the size of your skillet.
5. Fry the potato pancakes until they are golden brown and crispy on one side, about 3-4 minutes. Flip them over and fry the other side until it's also golden brown and crispy, another 3-4 minutes.
6. Once done, remove the Kartoffelpuffer from the skillet and place them on a plate lined with paper towels to drain any excess oil. Repeat the frying process with the remaining potato mixture.

Serve your Kartoffelpuffer hot:

7. You can serve Kartoffelpuffer with a dollop of sour cream or applesauce on the side if you like. These crispy potato pancakes are delicious on their own and make a fantastic side dish or snack.

Gulaschsuppe (Goulash Soup)

Servings: 6-8
Preparation Time: 30 minutes
Cooking Time: 1 hour 30 minutes
Ingredients:

- 2 tablespoons vegetable oil
- 2 pounds (about 900g) beef stew meat, cut into 1-inch cubes
- 2 onions, finely chopped
- 2 cloves garlic, minced
- 2 tablespoons sweet paprika
- 1 teaspoon caraway seeds (optional)
- 1 red bell pepper, diced
- 1 yellow bell pepper, diced
- 1 green bell pepper, diced
- 2 tablespoons tomato paste
- 6 cups beef broth
- 2 large potatoes, peeled and diced
- Salt and black pepper, to taste
- 1/4 cup sour cream (optional)
- Chopped fresh parsley, for garnish (optional)

Instructions:

Brown the Meat:

1. In a large soup pot, heat the vegetable oil over medium-high heat. Add the beef cubes and brown them on all sides, about 5-7 minutes. Remove the beef from the pot and set it aside.

Sauté the Aromatics:

2. In the same pot, add the chopped onions and garlic. Sauté them until they become soft and translucent, about 5 minutes.

Season and Add Vegetables:

3. Return the browned beef to the pot with the onions and garlic. Stir in the sweet paprika and caraway seeds (if using) to coat the meat evenly.
4. Add the diced red, yellow, and green bell peppers, and cook for another 3-4 minutes until they begin to soften.

Create the Goulash Base:

5. Stir in the tomato paste and cook for 2 minutes to enhance the flavors.
6. Pour in the beef broth and add the diced potatoes. Bring the mixture to a boil.

Simmer and Season:

7. Reduce the heat to low, cover the pot, and let the Gulaschsuppe simmer for about 1 hour, or until the beef is tender and the potatoes are cooked through.
8. Season the soup with salt and black pepper to taste. Adjust the

seasoning as needed.
Serve your Gulaschsuppe:
9. Ladle the piping hot Goulash Soup into bowls. If desired, swirl a spoonful of sour cream into each serving and garnish with chopped fresh parsley.

Brettljause (Cold Cuts Platter)

Servings: 4-6
Preparation Time: 15 minutes
Ingredients:
For the Cold Cuts Platter:
- A selection of cold cuts (e.g., ham, salami, and roast beef)
- Sliced Swiss cheese
- Sliced Austrian cheese (e.g., Bergkäse or Gouda)
- Sliced rye bread or crusty rolls
- Pickles or gherkins
- Sliced tomatoes
- Sliced cucumbers
- Radishes
- Fresh chives, for garnish (optional)

For the Mustard Sauce:
- 1/4 cup Dijon mustard
- 1/4 cup whole-grain mustard
- 2 tablespoons honey
- 2 tablespoons white wine vinegar
- Salt and black pepper, to taste

Instructions:
Assemble the Cold Cuts Platter:
1. Arrange the cold cuts, Swiss cheese, Austrian cheese, and sliced rye bread or rolls on a wooden cutting board or serving platter. Be creative with your arrangement.
2. Add pickles or gherkins, sliced tomatoes, sliced cucumbers, and radishes to the platter. These fresh vegetables add a refreshing contrast to the rich cold cuts and cheeses.
3. Optionally, garnish with fresh chives for a burst of color and flavor.

Prepare the Mustard Sauce:
4. In a small bowl, whisk together the Dijon mustard, whole-grain mustard, honey, and white wine vinegar until well combined.

Serve your Brettljause:
5. Place the Mustard Sauce in a small bowl on the platter or serve it on the side.
6. Invite everyone to assemble their own open-faced sandwiches or nibble on the cold cuts and cheese as desired. Spread some Mustard Sauce on the bread or use it as a dipping sauce for an authentic Austrian experience.

Obatzda (Bavarian Cheese Spread)

Servings: 4-6
Preparation Time: 15 minutes
Ingredients:
- 8 ounces (about 225g) Camembert cheese, at room temperature
- 4 ounces (about 115g) cream cheese, at room temperature
- 2 tablespoons unsalted butter, softened
- 1 small onion, finely chopped
- 1 teaspoon sweet paprika
- 1/2 teaspoon caraway seeds (optional)
- 1/2 teaspoon salt
- 1/4 teaspoon black pepper
- 1/4 cup beer (choose a wheat beer or a light lager)
- 2-3 tablespoons chives, finely chopped, for garnish
- Fresh pretzels, rye bread, or crackers, for serving

Instructions:
Prepare the Cheese Spread:
1. In a mixing bowl, combine the softened Camembert cheese, cream cheese, and softened butter. Use a fork or a hand mixer to blend them until smooth and creamy.
2. Stir in the finely chopped onion, sweet paprika, caraway seeds (if using), salt, and black pepper. Mix well to incorporate all the ingredients.
3. Gradually add the beer while continuing to mix. You can adjust the amount of beer to achieve your desired consistency. Some people prefer a thicker spread, while others like it a bit thinner.

Serve your Obatzda:
4. Transfer the Obatzda cheese spread to a serving bowl.
5. Garnish with finely chopped chives for added flavor and a pop of color.
6. Serve your Obatzda with fresh pretzels, slices of rye bread, or

crackers. It's a perfect accompaniment for a cozy evening get-together or as a tasty snack during Oktoberfest celebrations.

Pilzrahmsuppe (Creamy Mushroom Soup)

Servings: 4-6
Preparation Time: 30 minutes
Ingredients:

- 1 pound (about 450g) fresh mushrooms (button or cremini), cleaned and sliced
- 1 small onion, finely chopped
- 2 cloves garlic, minced
- 2 tablespoons unsalted butter
- 2 tablespoons all-purpose flour
- 4 cups chicken or vegetable broth
- 1 cup heavy cream
- 1/2 teaspoon dried thyme (or 1 teaspoon fresh thyme leaves)
- Salt and black pepper, to taste
- Fresh chives or parsley, chopped, for garnish (optional)

Instructions:
Sauté the Mushrooms:

1. In a large pot or Dutch oven, melt the butter over medium heat. Add the chopped onion and minced garlic. Sauté for 2-3 minutes until the onion is translucent and fragrant.
2. Add the sliced mushrooms to the pot and continue to cook, stirring occasionally, until the mushrooms have released their moisture and become browned and tender, about 8-10 minutes.

Create the Soup Base:

3. Sprinkle the flour over the mushrooms and stir to coat them evenly. Cook for 1-2 minutes to eliminate the raw flour taste.
4. Pour in the chicken or vegetable broth while stirring continuously to avoid lumps. Bring the mixture to a gentle simmer.

Simmer and Blend:

5. Let the soup simmer for about 10-15 minutes, allowing the flavors to meld together and the soup to thicken slightly.
6. Using an immersion blender or a countertop blender, carefully puree the soup until it reaches your desired consistency. If using a countertop blender, return the soup to the pot.

Add Cream and Season:

7. Stir in the heavy cream and dried thyme (or fresh thyme leaves if

using). Let the soup simmer for an additional 5 minutes, ensuring it's heated through.
8. Season the Pilzrahmsuppe with salt and black pepper to taste. Adjust the seasoning as needed.

Serve your Creamy Mushroom Soup:
9. Ladle the soup into bowls and garnish with chopped fresh chives or parsley if desired.
10. Enjoy your comforting and creamy Pilzrahmsuppe as a delightful appetizer or a comforting meal, especially during chilly days. Serve it with a slice of crusty bread for a satisfying experience.

SOUPS AND STEWS

Frittatensuppe (Pancake Soup)

Servings: 4
Preparation Time: 20 minutes
Cooking Time: 10 minutes
Ingredients:
For the Pancakes:
- 2 large eggs
- 1/2 cup all-purpose flour
- 1/2 cup milk
- A pinch of salt
- Butter or oil for frying

For the Soup:
- 6 cups beef or vegetable broth
- 1 carrot, peeled and finely diced
- 1 celery stalk, finely diced
- 1 small leek, cleaned and thinly sliced
- 2 tablespoons butter
- Salt and black pepper, to taste
- Fresh chives, chopped, for garnish (optional)

Instructions:
Prepare the Pancakes:
1. In a mixing bowl, whisk together the eggs, all-purpose flour, milk, and a pinch of salt until you have a smooth batter.

2. In a non-stick skillet over medium heat, melt a small amount of butter or heat a bit of oil. Pour a ladleful of the pancake batter into the skillet, swirling it to create a thin pancake. Cook for 1-2 minutes on each side until lightly golden. Repeat until you've used all the batter, stacking the cooked pancakes on a plate.
3. Once the pancakes have cooled slightly, roll them up and slice them thinly into strips. These pancake strips are the "Frittaten" and will be used to garnish the soup.

Prepare the Soup:
4. In a large pot, melt the butter over medium heat. Add the diced carrot, celery, and leek. Sauté for about 5 minutes until they begin to soften.
5. Pour in the beef or vegetable broth and bring the mixture to a gentle simmer. Let it simmer for about 10 minutes or until the vegetables are tender.
6. Season the soup with salt and black pepper to taste.

Serve your Frittatensuppe:
7. Ladle the hot soup into bowls.
8. Garnish each serving with a generous handful of the sliced pancake strips (Frittaten) and, if desired, a sprinkle of chopped fresh chives.

Leberknödelsuppe (Liver Dumpling Soup)

Servings: 4-6
Preparation Time: 30 minutes
Cooking Time: 20 minutes
Ingredients:
For the Liver Dumplings:
- 1/2 pound (about 225g) chicken or pork liver, cleaned and finely chopped
- 1 small onion, finely chopped
- 1/2 cup fresh breadcrumbs
- 2 tablespoons fresh parsley, finely chopped
- 1 egg
- 2 tablespoons milk
- Salt and black pepper, to taste
- A pinch of ground nutmeg (optional)
- Butter or oil for frying

For the Soup:

- 6 cups beef or vegetable broth
- 1 carrot, peeled and diced
- 1 celery stalk, diced
- 1 small leek, cleaned and sliced
- 2 tablespoons butter
- Salt and black pepper, to taste
- Fresh chives, chopped, for garnish (optional)

Instructions:
Prepare the Liver Dumplings:
1. In a skillet over medium heat, melt a small amount of butter or heat a bit of oil. Add the finely chopped onion and sauté for 2-3 minutes until translucent. Remove from heat and let it cool.
2. In a mixing bowl, combine the finely chopped liver, sautéed onions, fresh breadcrumbs, chopped parsley, egg, milk, salt, black pepper, and a pinch of ground nutmeg (if using). Mix until all the ingredients are well combined.
3. With wet hands, shape the mixture into small dumplings (about 1 inch in diameter) and set them aside.

Prepare the Soup:
4. In a large pot, melt the butter over medium heat. Add the diced carrot, celery, and sliced leek. Sauté for about 5 minutes until the vegetables start to soften.
5. Pour in the beef or vegetable broth and bring the mixture to a gentle simmer. Let it simmer for about 10 minutes or until the vegetables are tender.
6. Season the soup with salt and black pepper to taste.

Cook the Liver Dumplings:
7. Carefully add the liver dumplings to the simmering soup. Let them cook for about 8-10 minutes until they are firm and cooked through. The dumplings will float to the surface when done.

Serve your Leberknödelsuppe:
8. Ladle the hot soup into bowls, ensuring that each serving has a generous portion of liver dumplings.
9. If desired, garnish with chopped fresh chives for added flavor and a touch of green.

Kürbiscremesuppe (Pumpkin Cream Soup)

Servings: 4-6
Preparation Time: 30 minutes

Cooking Time: 30 minutes
Ingredients:
- 2 pounds (about 900g) pumpkin or butternut squash, peeled, seeded, and diced
- 1 small onion, chopped
- 2 cloves garlic, minced
- 2 tablespoons butter
- 4 cups vegetable or chicken broth
- 1/2 teaspoon ground cinnamon
- 1/4 teaspoon ground nutmeg
- 1/4 teaspoon ground ginger
- 1/2 cup heavy cream
- Salt and black pepper, to taste
- Fresh chives or pumpkin seeds, for garnish (optional)

Instructions:
Prepare the Pumpkin:
1. Start by peeling, seeding, and dicing the pumpkin or butternut squash.

Sauté the Vegetables:
2. In a large pot, melt the butter over medium heat. Add the chopped onion and minced garlic. Sauté for about 3-4 minutes until the onion becomes translucent and fragrant.
3. Add the diced pumpkin or butternut squash to the pot and continue to cook for another 5 minutes, stirring occasionally.

Simmer the Soup:
4. Pour in the vegetable or chicken broth, and add the ground cinnamon, ground nutmeg, and ground ginger. Stir well.
5. Bring the mixture to a simmer and let it cook for about 20-25 minutes, or until the pumpkin is tender and easily pierced with a fork.

Blend and Season:
6. Use an immersion blender or a countertop blender to puree the soup until it's smooth and velvety.
7. Return the soup to the pot (if you used a countertop blender) and stir in the heavy cream.
8. Season the Kürbiscremesuppe with salt and black pepper to taste. Adjust the seasoning as needed.

Serve your Pumpkin Cream Soup:
9. Ladle the hot soup into bowls.

10. Garnish with a sprinkle of fresh chives or pumpkin seeds if desired.

Rindsgulasch (Beef Goulash)

Servings: 4-6
Preparation Time: 20 minutes
Cooking Time: 2 hours
Ingredients:
- 2 pounds (about 900g) beef stew meat, cut into 1-inch cubes
- 2 large onions, finely chopped
- 2 cloves garlic, minced
- 2 tablespoons vegetable oil
- 2 tablespoons sweet paprika
- 1 teaspoon caraway seeds
- 1 teaspoon tomato paste
- 1 red bell pepper, diced
- 1 yellow bell pepper, diced
- 2 cups beef broth
- 1 cup water
- Salt and black pepper, to taste
- Sour cream, for garnish (optional)
- Chopped fresh parsley, for garnish (optional)

Instructions:
Brown the Beef:
1. In a large Dutch oven or heavy pot, heat the vegetable oil over medium-high heat. Add the cubed beef in batches and brown it on all sides. Remove the browned beef from the pot and set it aside.

Sauté the Aromatics:
2. In the same pot, add the chopped onions and minced garlic. Sauté for about 5 minutes until the onions are soft and translucent.

Create the Goulash Base:
3. Stir in the sweet paprika, caraway seeds, and tomato paste. Cook for an additional 2 minutes to develop the flavors.
4. Add the diced red and yellow bell peppers to the pot, and cook for another 3-4 minutes.

Simmer the Goulash:
5. Return the browned beef to the pot and mix everything together.

6. Pour in the beef broth and water. Bring the mixture to a simmer.
7. Reduce the heat to low, cover the pot, and let the Rindsgulasch simmer gently for about 1.5 to 2 hours, or until the beef is tender and the flavors have melded together. Stir occasionally and add more water if needed to maintain a thick, stew-like consistency.
8. Season the goulash with salt and black pepper to taste. Adjust the seasoning as needed.

Serve your Rindsgulasch:
9. Ladle the hot goulash into bowls.
10. If desired, top each serving with a dollop of sour cream and a sprinkle of chopped fresh parsley for added richness and flavor.

Kartoffelsuppe (Potato Soup)

Servings: 4-6
Preparation Time: 30 minutes
Cooking Time: 30 minutes
Ingredients:
- 4 large potatoes, peeled and diced
- 1 onion, finely chopped
- 2 cloves garlic, minced
- 2 tablespoons butter
- 4 cups chicken or vegetable broth
- 1 cup milk
- 1/2 cup heavy cream
- 2 bay leaves
- 1/2 teaspoon dried thyme (or 1 teaspoon fresh thyme leaves)
- Salt and black pepper, to taste
- Chopped fresh chives or parsley, for garnish (optional)

Instructions:

Sauté the Vegetables:
1. In a large pot, melt the butter over medium heat. Add the chopped onion and minced garlic. Sauté for about 3-4 minutes until the onion becomes translucent and fragrant.
2. Add the diced potatoes to the pot and cook for another 5 minutes, stirring occasionally.

Simmer the Soup:
3. Pour in the chicken or vegetable broth and add the bay leaves and dried thyme (or fresh thyme leaves). Stir well.
4. Bring the mixture to a simmer and let it cook for about 20-25

minutes or until the potatoes are tender when pierced with a fork.

Blend and Season:
5. Remove and discard the bay leaves.
6. Use an immersion blender or a countertop blender to puree the soup until it's smooth and creamy.
7. Return the soup to the pot (if you used a countertop blender).
8. Stir in the milk and heavy cream.
9. Season the Kartoffelsuppe with salt and black pepper to taste. Adjust the seasoning as needed.

Serve your Potato Soup:
10. Ladle the hot soup into bowls.
11. Garnish with chopped fresh chives or parsley if desired.

Gemüsesuppe (Vegetable Soup)

Servings: 4-6
Preparation Time: 15 minutes
Cooking Time: 30 minutes
Ingredients:
- 2 tablespoons olive oil
- 1 onion, finely chopped
- 2 cloves garlic, minced
- 2 carrots, peeled and diced
- 2 celery stalks, diced
- 2 potatoes, peeled and diced
- 1 leek, cleaned and sliced
- 6 cups vegetable broth
- 1 cup green beans, trimmed and chopped
- 1 cup peas (fresh or frozen)
- 1 cup corn kernels (fresh or frozen)
- 1 teaspoon dried thyme (or 1 tablespoon fresh thyme leaves)
- Salt and black pepper, to taste
- Chopped fresh parsley, for garnish (optional)

Instructions:
Sauté the Vegetables:
1. In a large pot, heat the olive oil over medium heat. Add the chopped onion and minced garlic. Sauté for about 3-4 minutes until the onion becomes translucent and fragrant.
2. Add the diced carrots, celery, potatoes, and sliced leek to the pot. Cook for another 5 minutes, stirring occasionally.

Simmer the Soup:
3. Pour in the vegetable broth and add the dried thyme (or fresh thyme leaves). Stir well.
4. Bring the mixture to a simmer and let it cook for about 20-25 minutes or until the vegetables are tender.

Add the Green Vegetables:
5. Add the chopped green beans, peas, and corn kernels to the pot.
6. Continue to simmer for an additional 5-10 minutes until the green vegetables are tender and the soup is well heated through.

Season and Serve:
7. Season the Gemüsesuppe with salt and black pepper to taste. Adjust the seasoning as needed.
8. Ladle the hot vegetable soup into bowls.
9. If desired, garnish each serving with chopped fresh parsley for a burst of color and freshness.

Hühnersuppe (Chicken Soup)

Servings: 4-6
Preparation Time: 15 minutes
Cooking Time: 1 hour 30 minutes
Ingredients:
- 1 whole chicken (about 3-4 pounds), rinsed and patted dry
- 2 carrots, peeled and chopped
- 2 celery stalks, chopped
- 1 onion, peeled and halved
- 2 cloves garlic, smashed
- 2 bay leaves
- 1 teaspoon dried thyme (or 1 tablespoon fresh thyme leaves)
- 8 cups water
- Salt and black pepper, to taste
- Wide egg noodles or rice, cooked (optional)
- Chopped fresh parsley, for garnish (optional)
- Lemon wedges, for serving (optional)

Instructions:

Prepare the Chicken Broth:
1. Place the whole chicken in a large pot and add the chopped carrots, celery, onion halves, smashed garlic cloves, bay leaves, and dried thyme.
2. Pour in the water, ensuring that the chicken is mostly covered.

3. Bring the mixture to a boil over high heat. Once it's boiling, reduce the heat to low, cover the pot, and let it simmer for about 1 hour, skimming off any impurities that rise to the surface.
4. After simmering, carefully remove the chicken from the pot and place it on a cutting board. Allow it to cool slightly before shredding the meat, discarding the skin and bones.

Strain the Broth:
5. Strain the broth through a fine-mesh sieve into another large pot or bowl. Discard the solids, including the vegetables and herbs.

Return the Shredded Chicken:
6. Return the shredded chicken to the strained broth in the pot.

Simmer and Season:
7. Place the pot back on the stove and heat it over medium-low heat. Let it simmer gently for about 10-15 minutes to reheat the chicken.
8. Season the Hühnersuppe with salt and black pepper to taste. Adjust the seasoning as needed.

Serve your Chicken Soup:
9. Ladle the hot chicken soup into bowls.
10. If desired, you can add cooked wide egg noodles or rice to each serving.
11. Garnish with chopped fresh parsley and serve with lemon wedges on the side for a zesty touch.

Linsensuppe (Lentil Soup)

Servings: 4-6
Preparation Time: 15 minutes
Cooking Time: 45 minutes
Ingredients:
- 1 cup dried brown or green lentils, rinsed and drained
- 1 onion, finely chopped
- 2 carrots, peeled and diced
- 2 celery stalks, diced
- 2 cloves garlic, minced
- 2 tablespoons olive oil
- 1 teaspoon ground cumin
- 1/2 teaspoon ground coriander
- 1/2 teaspoon smoked paprika
- 6 cups vegetable or chicken broth

- 1 bay leaf
- Salt and black pepper, to taste
- Juice of 1 lemon
- Fresh parsley, chopped, for garnish (optional)

Instructions:

Sauté the Vegetables:

1. In a large pot, heat the olive oil over medium heat. Add the finely chopped onion, diced carrots, diced celery, and minced garlic. Sauté for about 5 minutes until the vegetables begin to soften.

Add the Lentils and Spices:

2. Stir in the rinsed lentils, ground cumin, ground coriander, and smoked paprika. Cook for another 2 minutes to toast the spices and coat the lentils.

Simmer the Soup:

3. Pour in the vegetable or chicken broth and add the bay leaf. Stir well.
4. Bring the mixture to a boil, then reduce the heat to low, cover the pot, and let it simmer for about 30-35 minutes or until the lentils and vegetables are tender.

Season and Finish:

5. Remove and discard the bay leaf.
6. Season the Linsensuppe with salt and black pepper to taste.
7. Squeeze the juice of one lemon into the soup and stir to incorporate.

Serve your Lentil Soup:

8. Ladle the hot lentil soup into bowls.
9. If desired, garnish with chopped fresh parsley for a pop of color and freshness.

MAIN COURSES: MEAT

Wiener Schnitzel

Servings: 4
Preparation Time: 15 minutes
Cooking Time: 10 minutes
Ingredients:
- 4 veal or pork cutlets (about 4-6 ounces each), pounded to 1/4-inch thickness
- Salt and black pepper, to taste
- 1 cup all-purpose flour, for dredging
- 2 large eggs
- 2 cups breadcrumbs (preferably fresh)
- Vegetable oil, for frying
- Lemon wedges, for serving
- Fresh parsley, chopped, for garnish (optional)

Instructions:
Prepare the Cutlets:
1. Place each cutlet between two sheets of plastic wrap or parchment paper. Use a meat mallet or the bottom of a heavy skillet to gently pound the cutlets to an even 1/4-inch thickness.
2. Season the cutlets with salt and black pepper.

Dredge the Cutlets:
3. Set up a breading station with three shallow bowls. Place the flour in the first bowl, beat the eggs in the second bowl, and add

the breadcrumbs to the third bowl.
4. Dredge each cutlet first in the flour, shaking off any excess, then dip it into the beaten eggs, allowing any excess to drip off, and finally coat it with breadcrumbs, pressing gently to adhere. Repeat for all the cutlets.

Fry the Schnitzel:
5. In a large skillet, heat enough vegetable oil to cover the bottom of the pan over medium-high heat. You want about 1/4 inch of oil.
6. Once the oil is hot (around 350°F or 175°C), carefully add the breaded cutlets one at a time. Cook for about 3-4 minutes per side until they are golden brown and crispy. Be gentle when flipping them.
7. Remove the Schnitzel from the skillet and place them on paper towels to drain any excess oil.

Serve your Wiener Schnitzel:
8. Transfer the hot Schnitzel to serving plates.
9. Garnish with lemon wedges and, if desired, sprinkle with chopped fresh parsley.
10. Serve immediately, traditionally with a slice of lemon for that classic burst of flavor.

Schweinsbraten (Roast Pork)

Servings: 6-8
Preparation Time: 15 minutes
Cooking Time: 3 hours
Ingredients:
For the Pork:
- 4 pounds boneless pork roast (shoulder or butt)
- 2 cloves garlic, minced
- 2 tablespoons caraway seeds
- 2 teaspoons salt
- 1 teaspoon black pepper
- 1 tablespoon vegetable oil

For the Gravy:
- 1 onion, finely chopped
- 2 tablespoons all-purpose flour
- 1 cup beef or vegetable broth
- 1 cup dry white wine

- Salt and black pepper, to taste

Instructions:

Prepare the Pork:
1. Preheat your oven to 325°F (163°C).
2. In a small bowl, combine the minced garlic, caraway seeds, salt, and black pepper to create a spice rub.
3. Pat the pork roast dry with paper towels. Rub the spice mixture evenly all over the pork roast.
4. Heat the vegetable oil in a large ovenproof skillet or roasting pan over medium-high heat. Add the pork roast and sear it on all sides until it's nicely browned, about 5-7 minutes per side.

Roast the Schweinsbraten:
5. Once the pork is browned, remove it from the skillet or roasting pan and set it aside.
6. In the same skillet or roasting pan, add the chopped onion and sauté for about 3-4 minutes until it becomes translucent and fragrant.
7. Sprinkle the flour over the sautéed onions and stir to create a roux. Cook for another 2-3 minutes, stirring continuously to avoid burning the flour.
8. Slowly add the beef or vegetable broth and dry white wine to the skillet, stirring constantly to create a smooth gravy. Bring the mixture to a simmer.
9. Return the seared pork roast to the skillet or roasting pan. Cover it with a lid or aluminum foil.
10. Transfer the covered skillet or roasting pan to the preheated oven and roast for about 2.5 to 3 hours, or until the pork is tender and the internal temperature reaches 145°F (63°C).

Serve your Schweinsbraten:
11. Remove the roast from the oven and let it rest for about 10 minutes before slicing.
12. Slice the pork and serve it with the flavorful gravy.

Tafelspitz (Boiled Beef)

Servings: 4-6
Preparation Time: 15 minutes
Cooking Time: 2 hours 30 minutes
Ingredients:
- 3 pounds beef (such as rump or sirloin)

- 2 onions, peeled and halved
- 2 carrots, peeled and roughly chopped
- 2 celery stalks, roughly chopped
- 2 leeks, cleaned and roughly chopped
- 1 bouquet garni (a bundle of fresh herbs, typically containing parsley, thyme, and bay leaves)
- Salt, to taste
- Freshly ground black pepper, to taste
- Horseradish sauce, for serving
- Apple-Horseradish Sauce (Apfelkren), for serving (optional)

Instructions:
Prepare the Beef:
1. Place the beef in a large pot and add enough water to cover it.
2. Bring the water to a boil over high heat.
3. Once the water is boiling, remove the beef and discard the water. This helps remove impurities and ensures a clearer broth.

Boil the Beef:
4. Return the beef to the pot and add enough fresh water to cover it.
5. Add the halved onions, chopped carrots, chopped celery, chopped leeks, and bouquet garni to the pot.
6. Season the water with salt and black pepper to taste.
7. Bring the water to a simmer over medium-high heat. Once it simmers, reduce the heat to low, cover the pot, and let it cook gently for about 2 to 2.5 hours. The beef should be tender but not falling apart.

Serve your Tafelspitz:
8. Remove the beef from the pot and let it rest for a few minutes.
9. Slice the Tafelspitz into thin slices and arrange them on a platter.
10. Strain the broth and serve it as a clear soup before the main course.
11. Serve the Tafelspitz with horseradish sauce and, if desired, Apple-Horseradish Sauce (Apfelkren) for a traditional Austrian touch.

Hühnerfrikassee (Chicken Fricassee)

Servings: 4-6
Preparation Time: 20 minutes
Cooking Time: 45 minutes
Ingredients:

- 2 pounds chicken (a whole chicken cut into pieces, or boneless chicken thighs or breasts)
- Salt and black pepper, to taste
- 3 tablespoons butter
- 1 onion, finely chopped
- 2 carrots, peeled and diced
- 2 celery stalks, diced
- 1 leek, cleaned and sliced
- 1/4 cup all-purpose flour
- 4 cups chicken broth
- 1 bay leaf
- 1/2 cup heavy cream
- 1 cup frozen peas
- 1/2 cup pearl onions (frozen or fresh, peeled)
- 2 tablespoons chopped fresh parsley, for garnish
- Lemon wedges, for serving (optional)

Instructions:
Cook the Chicken:
1. Season the chicken pieces with salt and black pepper.
2. In a large pot or Dutch oven, melt 2 tablespoons of butter over medium-high heat. Add the chicken pieces and brown them on all sides. This should take about 5-7 minutes. Once browned, remove the chicken from the pot and set it aside.

Sauté the Vegetables:
3. In the same pot, add the remaining 1 tablespoon of butter. Add the chopped onion, diced carrots, diced celery, and sliced leek. Sauté for about 5 minutes until the vegetables are softened.

Create the Fricassee Base:
4. Sprinkle the flour over the sautéed vegetables and stir to create a roux. Cook for another 2-3 minutes, stirring constantly.
5. Gradually add the chicken broth while continuing to stir, ensuring there are no lumps in the sauce.
6. Return the browned chicken pieces to the pot, add the bay leaf, and bring the mixture to a simmer.
7. Reduce the heat to low, cover the pot, and let it cook for about 25-30 minutes, or until the chicken is fully cooked and tender.

Finish the Fricassee:
8. Remove the chicken pieces from the pot and set them aside.
9. Stir in the heavy cream, frozen peas, and pearl onions. Simmer

for another 5-7 minutes until the sauce thickens slightly and the vegetables are tender.
10. Return the chicken to the pot and heat through for a few minutes.

Serve your Hühnerfrikassee:
11. Discard the bay leaf.
12. Ladle the chicken fricassee onto serving plates, ensuring each serving has a mix of chicken, vegetables, and sauce.
13. Garnish with chopped fresh parsley and serve with lemon wedges if desired.

Kasnocken (Austrian Dumplings with Cheese)

Servings: 4
Preparation Time: 20 minutes
Cooking Time: 15 minutes
Ingredients:
For the Dumplings:
- 2 cups all-purpose flour
- 2 large eggs
- 1/2 cup water
- 1/2 teaspoon salt
- 1/4 teaspoon ground black pepper
- 1/4 teaspoon ground nutmeg
- 1/2 cup grated Emmental cheese (or any Swiss cheese)
- 1/2 cup grated Gouda cheese (or any mild cheese)
- 2 tablespoons chopped fresh chives (optional)
- 2 tablespoons butter, for serving

For the Topping:
- 1 onion, thinly sliced
- 2 tablespoons butter
- 1/2 cup grated cheese (use the same as in the dumplings)
- Fresh chives, chopped, for garnish (optional)

Instructions:
Prepare the Dumpling Dough:
1. In a mixing bowl, combine the all-purpose flour, eggs, water, salt, ground black pepper, and ground nutmeg. Mix until you have a smooth dough.
2. Stir in the grated Emmental and Gouda cheeses, and chopped fresh chives if desired. The dough should be somewhat sticky.

Form the Dumplings:
3. Bring a large pot of salted water to a boil.
4. While the water is heating, wet your hands and shape the dough into small dumplings about the size of a walnut or a ping pong ball. You can use a spoon to scoop out portions of the dough and shape them in your hands.

Boil the Dumplings:
5. Once the water is boiling, carefully drop the dumplings into the pot. They will sink to the bottom initially and then rise to the surface. This should take about 3-5 minutes. Once they've floated to the top, let them cook for another 2-3 minutes.
6. Using a slotted spoon, remove the cooked dumplings from the water and place them on a plate.

Prepare the Topping:
7. In a skillet, melt 2 tablespoons of butter over medium-high heat. Add the thinly sliced onion and sauté until they are caramelized and golden brown, about 5-7 minutes.

Serve your Kasnocken:
8. Arrange the cooked Kasnocken (Austrian cheese dumplings) on serving plates.
9. Spoon the caramelized onions over the dumplings.
10. Sprinkle grated cheese on top, allowing it to melt slightly from the heat of the dumplings and onions.
11. If desired, garnish with chopped fresh chives for added flavor and freshness.
12. Serve your Kasnocken hot, drizzled with a bit of melted butter, and enjoy this classic Austrian comfort dish!

Rindsrouladen (Beef Roulades)

Servings: 4-6
Preparation Time: 30 minutes
Cooking Time: 1 hour 30 minutes
Ingredients:
For the Roulades:
- 4-6 beef slices (thinly sliced round or sirloin steak, about 4x6 inches each)
- 4-6 slices bacon
- 4-6 dill pickles, sliced lengthwise into thin strips
- 1 onion, finely chopped

- 2 tablespoons Dijon mustard
- Salt and black pepper, to taste
- Toothpicks or kitchen twine

For the Gravy:
- 2 tablespoons vegetable oil
- 1 onion, chopped
- 2 carrots, chopped
- 2 celery stalks, chopped
- 2 cloves garlic, minced
- 1 tablespoon tomato paste
- 2 cups beef broth
- 1 cup red wine (optional)
- 2 bay leaves
- 1 teaspoon dried thyme (or 2 teaspoons fresh thyme leaves)
- Salt and black pepper, to taste

Instructions:

Prepare the Roulades:
1. Lay out the beef slices on a clean surface. Season each slice with salt and black pepper.
2. Spread a thin layer of Dijon mustard on each beef slice.
3. Place a slice of bacon on top of the mustard.
4. Add a few strips of dill pickle and some chopped onion on each slice.
5. Carefully roll up each beef slice, securing the filling with toothpicks or kitchen twine. Make sure the rolls are sealed to prevent the filling from falling out during cooking.

Sear the Roulades:
6. In a large skillet or Dutch oven, heat the vegetable oil over medium-high heat. Brown the beef roulades on all sides, about 3-4 minutes per side. Remove them from the skillet and set them aside.

Prepare the Gravy:
7. In the same skillet, add the chopped onion, carrots, and celery. Sauté for about 5 minutes until the vegetables are softened.
8. Stir in the minced garlic and tomato paste. Cook for an additional 2 minutes.
9. Pour in the beef broth and red wine (if using), and add the bay leaves and dried thyme. Bring the mixture to a simmer.
10. Return the seared beef roulades to the skillet. Cover the skillet,

reduce the heat to low, and let it simmer gently for about 1 hour. The beef should become tender.
11. Occasionally check and turn the roulades during simmering to ensure even cooking.

Serve your Rindsrouladen:
12. Once the beef roulades are tender, remove them from the skillet and keep them warm.
13. If the gravy needs thickening, you can remove the bay leaves and simmer it uncovered for a few more minutes until it reaches your desired consistency.
14. Slice the roulades into rounds and serve them with the flavorful gravy.

Rahmschnitzel (Creamy Pork Schnitzel)

Servings: 4
Preparation Time: 20 minutes
Cooking Time: 20 minutes
Ingredients:
For the Pork Schnitzel:
- 4 pork loin or pork tenderloin medallions (about 4-6 ounces each)
- Salt and black pepper, to taste
- 1 cup all-purpose flour, for dredging
- 2 large eggs
- 2 cups breadcrumbs (preferably fresh)
- 2 tablespoons vegetable oil, for frying

For the Creamy Sauce:
- 2 tablespoons butter
- 1 onion, finely chopped
- 2 cloves garlic, minced
- 1 cup heavy cream
- 1/2 cup chicken broth
- 1 tablespoon Dijon mustard
- 1 tablespoon fresh lemon juice
- 1/4 cup chopped fresh parsley
- Salt and black pepper, to taste
- Lemon wedges, for serving (optional)

Instructions:
Prepare the Pork Schnitzel:

1. Season each pork medallion with salt and black pepper.
2. Set up a breading station with three shallow bowls. Place the flour in the first bowl, beat the eggs in the second bowl, and add the breadcrumbs to the third bowl.
3. Dredge each pork medallion first in the flour, shaking off any excess, then dip it into the beaten eggs, allowing any excess to drip off, and finally coat it with breadcrumbs, pressing gently to adhere. Repeat for all the medallions.

Fry the Pork Schnitzel:

4. In a large skillet, heat the vegetable oil over medium-high heat. You want enough oil to cover the bottom of the pan.
5. Once the oil is hot, carefully add the breaded pork medallions one at a time. Cook for about 3-4 minutes per side until they are golden brown and crispy. Be gentle when flipping them.
6. Remove the schnitzel from the skillet and place them on paper towels to drain any excess oil.

Prepare the Creamy Sauce:

7. In the same skillet, melt the butter over medium heat. Add the finely chopped onion and minced garlic. Sauté for about 3-4 minutes until the onion becomes translucent and fragrant.
8. Pour in the heavy cream, chicken broth, Dijon mustard, and fresh lemon juice. Stir well to combine.
9. Bring the mixture to a gentle simmer and let it cook for about 5 minutes until the sauce thickens slightly.
10. Season the creamy sauce with salt and black pepper to taste. Adjust the seasoning as needed.

Serve your Rahmschnitzel:

11. Ladle the creamy sauce over the cooked pork schnitzel.
12. Garnish with chopped fresh parsley and serve with lemon wedges if desired.

Faschierter Braten (Austrian Meatloaf)

Servings: 6-8
Preparation Time: 20 minutes
Cooking Time: 1 hour 15 minutes
Ingredients:
For the Meatloaf:
- 1 1/2 pounds ground beef (or a mixture of beef and pork)
- 1 cup fresh breadcrumbs

- 1/2 cup milk
- 1 onion, finely chopped
- 2 cloves garlic, minced
- 2 eggs
- 2 tablespoons vegetable oil
- 1/4 cup fresh parsley, chopped
- 1/2 teaspoon salt
- 1/4 teaspoon black pepper
- 1/4 teaspoon ground nutmeg
- 1/4 teaspoon paprika

For the Sauce:
- 1 onion, finely chopped
- 2 tablespoons butter
- 2 tablespoons all-purpose flour
- 1 1/2 cups beef broth
- 1/2 cup heavy cream
- 1/2 teaspoon dried thyme (or 1 teaspoon fresh thyme leaves)
- Salt and black pepper, to taste
- Fresh parsley, chopped, for garnish (optional)

Instructions:

Prepare the Meatloaf:

1. Preheat your oven to 350°F (175°C).
2. In a mixing bowl, combine the fresh breadcrumbs and milk. Let them soak for a few minutes until the breadcrumbs absorb the milk.
3. In a skillet, heat the vegetable oil over medium heat. Add the finely chopped onion and minced garlic. Sauté for about 3-4 minutes until the onion becomes translucent and fragrant. Remove from heat and let it cool.
4. In a large mixing bowl, combine the ground beef, soaked breadcrumbs, sautéed onion and garlic, eggs, chopped fresh parsley, salt, black pepper, ground nutmeg, and paprika. Mix well until all the ingredients are thoroughly combined.
5. Shape the meat mixture into a loaf and place it in a greased baking dish.

Bake the Meatloaf:

6. Bake the meatloaf in the preheated oven for about 1 hour or until it's cooked through and the top is browned.

Prepare the Sauce:

7. In a skillet, melt the butter over medium heat. Add the finely chopped onion and sauté until it becomes translucent, about 3-4 minutes.
8. Stir in the all-purpose flour and cook for another 2 minutes to create a roux.
9. Gradually add the beef broth and heavy cream, stirring constantly to create a smooth sauce.
10. Add the dried thyme (or fresh thyme leaves) and season the sauce with salt and black pepper to taste. Simmer for about 5 minutes until the sauce thickens slightly.

Serve your Faschierter Braten:
11. Slice the meatloaf and serve it with the creamy sauce drizzled over the top.
12. If desired, garnish with chopped fresh parsley for a burst of color and freshness.

Hirschbraten (Venison Roast)

Servings: 6-8
Preparation Time: 20 minutes
Cooking Time: 2 hours
Ingredients:
For the Venison Roast:
- 3-4 pounds venison roast (shoulder or loin)
- Salt and black pepper, to taste
- 2 tablespoons vegetable oil
- 1 onion, chopped
- 2 carrots, chopped
- 2 celery stalks, chopped
- 2 cloves garlic, minced
- 2 sprigs fresh rosemary (or 1 teaspoon dried rosemary)
- 2 sprigs fresh thyme (or 1 teaspoon dried thyme)
- 2 bay leaves
- 1 cup red wine
- 1 cup beef broth

For the Gravy:
- 2 tablespoons butter
- 2 tablespoons all-purpose flour
- Salt and black pepper, to taste

Instructions:

Prepare the Venison Roast:
1. Preheat your oven to 325°F (163°C).
2. Season the venison roast generously with salt and black pepper.
3. In a large ovenproof skillet or Dutch oven, heat the vegetable oil over medium-high heat. Add the venison roast and sear it on all sides until it's nicely browned, about 5-7 minutes per side. Remove it from the skillet and set it aside.

Sauté the Vegetables:
4. In the same skillet, add the chopped onion, carrots, and celery. Sauté for about 5 minutes until the vegetables are softened.
5. Stir in the minced garlic and cook for an additional minute until fragrant.

Roast the Venison:
6. Return the seared venison roast to the skillet.
7. Add the fresh rosemary, fresh thyme, bay leaves, red wine, and beef broth to the skillet.
8. Cover the skillet or Dutch oven with a lid or aluminum foil.
9. Transfer the covered skillet or Dutch oven to the preheated oven and roast for about 1.5 to 2 hours, or until the venison is cooked to your desired level of doneness. A meat thermometer should read 145°F (63°C) for medium-rare or 160°F (71°C) for medium.

Prepare the Gravy:
10. Once the venison is done, remove it from the skillet and let it rest for about 10 minutes before slicing.
11. In the same skillet, melt the butter over medium heat. Stir in the all-purpose flour and cook for about 2 minutes to create a roux.
12. Gradually add the cooking juices from the skillet while stirring constantly to create a smooth gravy. Cook for another 5 minutes until the gravy thickens. Season with salt and black pepper to taste.

Serve your Hirschbraten:
13. Slice the venison roast and arrange it on a platter.
14. Drizzle the rich gravy over the sliced venison.

Gefüllte Paprika (Stuffed Peppers)

Servings: 4-6
Preparation Time: 30 minutes
Cooking Time: 45 minutes
Ingredients:

For the Stuffed Peppers:
- 6 large bell peppers (red, yellow, or green)
- 1 pound ground beef (or a mixture of beef and pork)
- 1 cup cooked rice
- 1 onion, finely chopped
- 2 cloves garlic, minced
- 1/2 cup canned diced tomatoes
- 1/4 cup fresh parsley, chopped
- Salt and black pepper, to taste
- 1/2 teaspoon paprika
- 1/2 teaspoon dried oregano (or 1 teaspoon fresh oregano leaves)
- 1/2 cup grated Parmesan cheese (optional)
- 2 tablespoons olive oil

For the Tomato Sauce:
- 1 can (14 ounces) crushed tomatoes
- 1/2 cup water
- 1/2 teaspoon sugar
- Salt and black pepper, to taste
- 1/2 teaspoon dried basil (or 1 teaspoon fresh basil leaves)
- 1/2 teaspoon dried thyme (or 1 teaspoon fresh thyme leaves)

Instructions:

Prepare the Stuffed Peppers:

1. Preheat your oven to 350°F (175°C).
2. Cut the tops off the bell peppers and remove the seeds and membranes from the inside. Rinse them thoroughly.
3. In a skillet, heat olive oil over medium-high heat. Add the chopped onion and minced garlic. Sauté for about 3-4 minutes until the onion becomes translucent and fragrant.
4. Add the ground beef (or beef and pork mixture) to the skillet. Cook, breaking it up with a spoon, until it's browned and cooked through.
5. Stir in the cooked rice, canned diced tomatoes, fresh parsley, salt, black pepper, paprika, and dried oregano. Cook for another 2-3 minutes until everything is well combined.
6. If desired, mix in grated Parmesan cheese for extra flavor.

Stuff and Bake the Peppers:

7. Carefully stuff each bell pepper with the meat and rice mixture, pressing it down gently to ensure they are well-filled.
8. Place the stuffed peppers in a baking dish.

Prepare the Tomato Sauce:
9. In a separate bowl, combine the crushed tomatoes, water, sugar, salt, black pepper, dried basil, and dried thyme. Mix well.

Bake the Stuffed Peppers:
10. Pour the tomato sauce over the stuffed peppers in the baking dish.
11. Cover the dish with aluminum foil.
12. Bake in the preheated oven for about 35-40 minutes, or until the peppers are tender.
13. Remove the foil and bake for an additional 5-10 minutes until the tops of the peppers are slightly browned.

Serve your Gefüllte Paprika:
14. Carefully transfer the stuffed peppers to serving plates.
15. Spoon some of the tomato sauce over each pepper.

MAIN COURSES: SEAFOOD AND VEGETARIAN

Forelle Müllerin (Trout with Brown Butter)

Servings: 4
Preparation Time: 20 minutes
Cooking Time: 15 minutes
Ingredients:
For the Trout:
- 4 whole trout, cleaned and gutted
- Salt and black pepper, to taste
- All-purpose flour, for dusting
- 4 tablespoons vegetable oil, for frying

For the Brown Butter Sauce:
- 1/2 cup (1 stick) unsalted butter
- 2 tablespoons fresh lemon juice
- 2 tablespoons fresh parsley, chopped
- 1/4 cup sliced almonds (optional, for garnish)
- Lemon wedges, for serving

Instructions:
Prepare the Trout:
1. Rinse the trout inside and out under cold running water. Pat them dry with paper towels.
2. Season the trout inside and out with salt and black pepper.
3. Lightly dust each trout with all-purpose flour, shaking off any

excess.

Pan-Fry the Trout:
4. In a large skillet, heat the vegetable oil over medium-high heat.
5. Carefully add the trout to the skillet. Depending on the size of your skillet, you may need to cook them in batches.
6. Cook the trout for about 3-4 minutes on each side until they are golden brown and the flesh flakes easily when tested with a fork. The cooking time may vary depending on the size of the trout.
7. Remove the trout from the skillet and place them on a serving platter. Keep them warm.

Prepare the Brown Butter Sauce:
8. In the same skillet, melt the unsalted butter over medium heat. Continue to cook the butter, swirling the skillet occasionally, until it turns a golden brown color and has a nutty aroma. Be careful not to burn it; this should take about 3-4 minutes.
9. Once the butter is browned, remove it from the heat and immediately stir in the fresh lemon juice and chopped fresh parsley.

Serve your Forelle Müllerin:
10. Spoon the brown butter sauce over the pan-fried trout.
11. If desired, garnish with sliced almonds for added texture and lemon wedges for an extra burst of freshness.

Lachs in Dillsoße (Salmon in Dill Sauce)

Servings: 4
Preparation Time: 15 minutes
Cooking Time: 20 minutes
Ingredients:
For the Salmon:
- 4 salmon fillets (about 6 ounces each)
- Salt and black pepper, to taste
- 2 tablespoons olive oil
- 1 lemon, thinly sliced

For the Dill Sauce:
- 2 tablespoons unsalted butter
- 2 tablespoons all-purpose flour
- 1 1/2 cups milk
- 1/4 cup fresh dill, chopped
- 2 tablespoons fresh lemon juice

- 1 teaspoon lemon zest
- Salt and black pepper, to taste

Instructions:

Prepare the Salmon:
1. Season the salmon fillets with salt and black pepper on both sides.
2. In a large skillet, heat the olive oil over medium-high heat.
3. Add the salmon fillets to the skillet and cook for about 3-4 minutes on each side, or until they are browned on the outside and flake easily with a fork. Cooking time may vary depending on the thickness of the fillets.
4. While cooking, place a few lemon slices on top of each salmon fillet to infuse the citrus flavor.
5. Once the salmon is cooked to your desired level of doneness, remove them from the skillet and keep them warm.

Prepare the Dill Sauce:
6. In the same skillet, melt the unsalted butter over medium heat.
7. Stir in the all-purpose flour to create a roux. Cook for about 1-2 minutes, stirring constantly.
8. Gradually add the milk to the roux, whisking constantly to create a smooth sauce. Continue to cook and whisk until the sauce thickens, about 3-4 minutes.
9. Stir in the chopped fresh dill, fresh lemon juice, and lemon zest.
10. Season the dill sauce with salt and black pepper to taste. Adjust the seasoning as needed.

Serve your Lachs in Dillsoße:
11. Spoon the dill sauce over the cooked salmon fillets.
12. Garnish with extra fresh dill and lemon slices if desired.

Kartoffelstrudel (Potato Strudel)

Servings: 4-6
Preparation Time: 30 minutes
Cooking Time: 30 minutes
Ingredients:

For the Potato Filling:
- 4 large potatoes, peeled and diced
- 1 onion, finely chopped
- 2 cloves garlic, minced
- 2 tablespoons vegetable oil

- 1/2 cup sour cream
- 1/2 cup grated Emmental cheese (or any Swiss cheese)
- 1/4 cup fresh parsley, chopped
- Salt and black pepper, to taste

For the Strudel Dough:

- 1 package (about 16 ounces) phyllo dough, thawed
- 1/2 cup unsalted butter, melted

Instructions:

Prepare the Potato Filling:

1. Place the diced potatoes in a large pot of salted water. Bring to a boil and cook until the potatoes are tender when pierced with a fork, about 10-12 minutes. Drain and set aside.
2. In a skillet, heat the vegetable oil over medium-high heat. Add the finely chopped onion and minced garlic. Sauté for about 3-4 minutes until the onion becomes translucent and fragrant.
3. In a large mixing bowl, combine the cooked potatoes, sautéed onion and garlic, sour cream, grated Emmental cheese, and chopped fresh parsley. Mix well.
4. Season the potato filling with salt and black pepper to taste. Adjust the seasoning as needed.

Assemble the Potato Strudel:

5. Preheat your oven to 350°F (175°C).
6. Lay out one sheet of phyllo dough on a clean surface and brush it with melted butter. Place another sheet of phyllo dough on top and repeat the process until you have a stack of 4-6 sheets, brushing each sheet with butter.
7. Spoon half of the potato filling along one of the long edges of the phyllo dough stack, leaving about 2 inches of dough on either side. Roll up the phyllo dough and filling like a burrito, folding in the sides as you go.
8. Repeat the process with the remaining phyllo dough sheets and potato filling to make a second strudel.

Bake the Potato Strudel:

9. Place both potato strudels on a baking sheet lined with parchment paper.
10. Brush the tops of the strudels with the remaining melted butter.
11. Bake in the preheated oven for about 20-30 minutes, or until the strudels are golden brown and crisp.

Serve your Kartoffelstrudel:

12. Remove the potato strudels from the oven and let them cool slightly before slicing.
13. Slice the strudels into portions and serve warm.

Gemüsestrudel (Vegetable Strudel)

Servings: 4-6
Preparation Time: 30 minutes
Cooking Time: 30 minutes
Ingredients:
For the Vegetable Filling:
- 2 tablespoons olive oil
- 1 onion, finely chopped
- 2 cloves garlic, minced
- 2 cups mixed vegetables (e.g., bell peppers, zucchini, carrots, and spinach), diced or sliced
- 1 cup mushrooms, sliced
- 1/2 cup cooked and chopped spinach (squeeze out excess moisture)
- 1/2 cup grated Gruyère cheese (or any Swiss cheese)
- 1/4 cup fresh parsley, chopped
- Salt and black pepper, to taste

For the Strudel Dough:
- 1 package (about 16 ounces) phyllo dough, thawed
- 1/2 cup unsalted butter, melted

Instructions:
Prepare the Vegetable Filling:
1. In a large skillet, heat the olive oil over medium-high heat. Add the finely chopped onion and minced garlic. Sauté for about 3-4 minutes until the onion becomes translucent and fragrant.
2. Add the diced or sliced mixed vegetables and mushrooms to the skillet. Sauté for about 5-7 minutes until the vegetables are tender.
3. Stir in the cooked and chopped spinach, grated Gruyère cheese, and chopped fresh parsley. Mix well.
4. Season the vegetable filling with salt and black pepper to taste. Adjust the seasoning as needed.

Assemble the Vegetable Strudel:
5. Preheat your oven to 350°F (175°C).
6. Lay out one sheet of phyllo dough on a clean surface and brush it

with melted butter. Place another sheet of phyllo dough on top and repeat the process until you have a stack of 4-6 sheets, brushing each sheet with butter.
7. Spoon half of the vegetable filling along one of the long edges of the phyllo dough stack, leaving about 2 inches of dough on either side. Roll up the phyllo dough and filling like a burrito, folding in the sides as you go.
8. Repeat the process with the remaining phyllo dough sheets and vegetable filling to make a second strudel.

Bake the Vegetable Strudel:
9. Place both vegetable strudels on a baking sheet lined with parchment paper.
10. Brush the tops of the strudels with the remaining melted butter.
11. Bake in the preheated oven for about 20-30 minutes, or until the strudels are golden brown and crisp.

Serve your Gemüsestrudel:
12. Remove the vegetable strudels from the oven and let them cool slightly before slicing.
13. Slice the strudels into portions and serve warm.

Kürbisrisotto (Pumpkin Risotto)

Servings: 4-6
Preparation Time: 10 minutes
Cooking Time: 30 minutes
Ingredients:
For the Pumpkin Purée:
- 2 cups diced pumpkin (butternut squash or any sweet variety)
- 1 tablespoon olive oil
- Salt and black pepper, to taste

For the Risotto:
- 2 cups Arborio rice
- 4 cups vegetable broth (or chicken broth)
- 1 onion, finely chopped
- 2 cloves garlic, minced
- 1/2 cup dry white wine (optional)
- 1/2 cup grated Parmesan cheese
- 2 tablespoons butter
- 1/4 cup fresh parsley, chopped
- Salt and black pepper, to taste

Instructions:
Prepare the Pumpkin Purée:
1. Preheat your oven to 400°F (200°C).
2. Toss the diced pumpkin with olive oil, salt, and black pepper in a baking dish.
3. Roast the pumpkin in the preheated oven for about 20-25 minutes, or until it's tender and slightly caramelized. Remove from the oven and let it cool slightly.
4. Using a blender or food processor, puree the roasted pumpkin until smooth. Set aside.

Prepare the Risotto:
5. In a large skillet or saucepan, heat the vegetable broth over low heat. Keep it warm but not boiling.
6. In a separate large skillet or saucepan, melt the butter over medium heat. Add the finely chopped onion and sauté for about 3-4 minutes until it becomes translucent and fragrant.
7. Stir in the minced garlic and cook for an additional minute until fragrant.
8. Add the Arborio rice to the skillet and cook for about 2-3 minutes, stirring constantly, until the rice grains are well-coated with butter and slightly translucent around the edges.
9. If using, pour in the dry white wine and cook until it's mostly absorbed by the rice.
10. Begin adding the warm vegetable broth, one ladle at a time, stirring constantly and allowing each addition to be absorbed before adding more. Continue this process until the rice is creamy and tender, which should take about 18-20 minutes.
11. Stir in the pumpkin purée and continue to cook for another 2-3 minutes, until the risotto is heated through.
12. Remove the risotto from heat and stir in the grated Parmesan cheese and fresh parsley.
13. Season the risotto with salt and black pepper to taste. Adjust the seasoning as needed.

Serve your Kürbisrisotto:
14. Spoon the creamy pumpkin risotto onto serving plates.
15. Garnish with extra Parmesan cheese and a sprinkle of fresh parsley, if desired.

Schwammerlragout (Mushroom Ragout)

Servings: 4
Preparation Time: 15 minutes
Cooking Time: 25 minutes
Ingredients:

- 1 pound fresh mushrooms (such as white button or cremini), cleaned and sliced
- 1 onion, finely chopped
- 2 cloves garlic, minced
- 2 tablespoons butter
- 2 tablespoons all-purpose flour
- 1 cup vegetable broth
- 1/2 cup heavy cream
- 1/4 cup dry white wine (optional)
- 2 tablespoons fresh parsley, chopped
- Salt and black pepper, to taste

Instructions:

Prepare the Mushroom Ragout:

1. In a large skillet, melt the butter over medium-high heat.
2. Add the finely chopped onion and minced garlic. Sauté for about 3-4 minutes until the onion becomes translucent and fragrant.
3. Stir in the sliced mushrooms and cook for another 5-7 minutes until they release their moisture and start to brown.
4. Sprinkle the all-purpose flour over the mushroom mixture and stir well to combine. Cook for 2-3 minutes to remove the raw taste of the flour.
5. If using, pour in the dry white wine and cook until it's mostly absorbed by the mushroom mixture.
6. Gradually add the vegetable broth, stirring constantly to create a smooth sauce.
7. Reduce the heat to low and let the mushroom ragout simmer for about 10 minutes, allowing the flavors to meld and the sauce to thicken slightly.
8. Stir in the heavy cream and continue to simmer for another 5 minutes until the sauce is creamy and the mushrooms are tender.
9. Season the mushroom ragout with salt and black pepper to taste. Adjust the seasoning as needed.

Serve your Schwammerlragout:

10. Spoon the mushroom ragout onto serving plates.

11. Garnish with chopped fresh parsley for a burst of color and freshness.

Potato Dumplings with Mushroom Sauce

Servings: 4
Preparation Time: 30 minutes
Cooking Time: 30 minutes
Ingredients:
For the Potato Dumplings (Kartoffelknödel):
- 4 large potatoes, peeled and quartered
- 1/2 cup all-purpose flour
- 1/4 cup semolina flour
- 1 egg
- Salt, to taste
- Ground nutmeg, to taste (optional)

For the Mushroom Sauce (Pilzsauce):
- 1 pound fresh mushrooms (such as cremini or white button), sliced
- 1 onion, finely chopped
- 2 cloves garlic, minced
- 2 tablespoons butter
- 1 cup vegetable broth
- 1/2 cup heavy cream
- 2 tablespoons fresh parsley, chopped
- Salt and black pepper, to taste

Instructions:
Prepare the Potato Dumplings:
1. Place the peeled and quartered potatoes in a large pot of salted water. Bring to a boil and cook until the potatoes are fork-tender, about 15-20 minutes.
2. Drain the cooked potatoes and let them cool slightly.
3. Mash the potatoes while they are still warm until you have smooth, lump-free mashed potatoes.
4. In a mixing bowl, combine the mashed potatoes, all-purpose flour, semolina flour, egg, salt, and ground nutmeg (if using). Mix well until the dough comes together.
5. Divide the dough into 4 equal portions and shape each portion into a ball. Then, flatten each ball slightly to form dumplings.

Cook the Potato Dumplings:

6. In a large pot of boiling salted water, carefully add the potato dumplings. Reduce the heat to a gentle simmer and cook the dumplings for about 20-25 minutes, or until they float to the surface and are cooked through.
7. Using a slotted spoon, remove the cooked dumplings from the water and drain them on a plate lined with paper towels. Keep them warm.

Prepare the Mushroom Sauce:
8. In a large skillet, melt the butter over medium-high heat.
9. Add the finely chopped onion and minced garlic. Sauté for about 3-4 minutes until the onion becomes translucent and fragrant.
10. Stir in the sliced mushrooms and cook for another 5-7 minutes until they release their moisture and start to brown.
11. Pour in the vegetable broth and heavy cream. Stir well and let the sauce simmer for about 10-15 minutes until it thickens and the mushrooms are tender.
12. Season the mushroom sauce with salt and black pepper to taste. Adjust the seasoning as needed.

Serve your Kartoffelknödel mit Pilzsauce:
13. Place the warm potato dumplings on serving plates.
14. Spoon the mushroom sauce over the dumplings.
15. Garnish with chopped fresh parsley for a burst of color and freshness.

Kartoffel-Gemüse Gratin (Potato and Vegetable Gratin)

Servings: 4-6
Preparation Time: 20 minutes
Cooking Time: 1 hour
Ingredients:
For the Gratin:
- 4 large potatoes, peeled and thinly sliced
- 2 carrots, peeled and thinly sliced
- 2 zucchini, thinly sliced
- 1 onion, thinly sliced
- 2 cloves garlic, minced
- 1 cup grated Gruyère cheese (or any Swiss cheese)
- 2 tablespoons fresh thyme leaves

- Salt and black pepper, to taste

For the Cream Sauce:
- 2 cups heavy cream
- 2 tablespoons butter
- 2 tablespoons all-purpose flour
- 1/4 teaspoon ground nutmeg
- Salt and black pepper, to taste

Instructions:

Prepare the Gratin:
1. Preheat your oven to 375°F (190°C).
2. In a large mixing bowl, combine the thinly sliced potatoes, carrots, zucchini, onion, and minced garlic.
3. Add the grated Gruyère cheese and fresh thyme leaves to the vegetable mixture. Season with salt and black pepper to taste. Toss everything together to evenly distribute the ingredients.

Prepare the Cream Sauce:
4. In a saucepan, melt the butter over medium heat.
5. Stir in the all-purpose flour to create a roux. Cook for about 1-2 minutes, stirring constantly, to remove the raw taste of the flour.
6. Gradually add the heavy cream to the roux, whisking constantly to create a smooth sauce.
7. Season the cream sauce with ground nutmeg, salt, and black pepper to taste. Continue to cook and whisk until the sauce thickens, about 5-7 minutes. Remove it from heat.

Assemble and Bake the Gratin:
8. Grease a large ovenproof baking dish.
9. Arrange a layer of the potato and vegetable mixture in the bottom of the baking dish.
10. Pour a portion of the cream sauce over the vegetables.
11. Repeat the layers until all the vegetables and sauce are used up, finishing with a layer of sauce on top.

Bake the Gratin:
12. Cover the baking dish with aluminum foil.
13. Bake in the preheated oven for about 40-45 minutes, or until the vegetables are tender.
14. Remove the foil and continue to bake for an additional 15-20 minutes, or until the top is golden brown and bubbly.

Serve your Kartoffel-Gemüse Gratin:
15. Let the gratin cool for a few minutes before serving.

16. Scoop out portions onto serving plates.

Käsespätzle (Cheese Spaetzle)

Servings: 4-6
Preparation Time: 20 minutes
Cooking Time: 20 minutes
Ingredients:
For the Spaetzle:
- 2 cups all-purpose flour
- 4 large eggs
- 1/2 cup water
- 1/2 teaspoon salt
- 1/4 teaspoon ground nutmeg

For the Cheese Sauce:
- 2 cups grated Emmental cheese (or Gruyère cheese)
- 1/2 cup grated Parmesan cheese
- 1 cup heavy cream
- 2 tablespoons unsalted butter
- Salt and black pepper, to taste
- Fresh chives, chopped (for garnish, optional)

Instructions:
Prepare the Spaetzle:
1. In a mixing bowl, combine the all-purpose flour, eggs, water, salt, and ground nutmeg. Mix until you have a smooth, thick batter. Let it rest for about 10 minutes.
2. Bring a large pot of salted water to a boil.
3. Using a spaetzle maker or a large-holed colander, press the batter through the holes directly into the boiling water. The spaetzle should drop into the water and cook for about 2-3 minutes or until they float to the surface.
4. Using a slotted spoon, transfer the cooked spaetzle to a colander to drain. Repeat the process until all the batter is used.

Prepare the Cheese Sauce:
5. In a large skillet, melt the unsalted butter over medium heat.
6. Add the cooked spaetzle to the skillet and cook for about 2-3 minutes, stirring gently to lightly brown the spaetzle.
7. Pour in the heavy cream and bring the mixture to a gentle simmer.
8. Reduce the heat to low, and gradually stir in the grated Emmental

cheese and grated Parmesan cheese. Continue to stir until the cheese is melted and the sauce is smooth.
9. Season the cheese sauce with salt and black pepper to taste. Adjust the seasoning as needed.

Serve your Käsespätzle:
10. Spoon the creamy cheese spaetzle onto serving plates.
11. Garnish with chopped fresh chives, if desired.

Krautfleckerl (Cabbage Pasta)

Servings: 4-6
Preparation Time: 15 minutes
Cooking Time: 25 minutes
Ingredients:
- 12 ounces (about 350 grams) egg noodles or any short pasta of your choice
- 1 small green cabbage, shredded
- 1 onion, finely chopped
- 2 cloves garlic, minced
- 2 tablespoons vegetable oil
- 2 tablespoons unsalted butter
- 1 teaspoon caraway seeds (optional)
- Salt and black pepper, to taste
- Fresh parsley, chopped (for garnish, optional)
- Sour cream, for serving (optional)

Instructions:
Prepare the Pasta:
1. Cook the egg noodles or short pasta according to the package instructions until they are al dente. Drain and set aside.

Prepare the Cabbage Mixture:
2. In a large skillet, heat the vegetable oil and melt the butter over medium-high heat.
3. Add the finely chopped onion and minced garlic. Sauté for about 3-4 minutes until the onion becomes translucent and fragrant.
4. If using, sprinkle the caraway seeds into the skillet and toast them for about a minute to release their flavor.
5. Add the shredded cabbage to the skillet. Sauté for about 10-15 minutes, stirring occasionally, until the cabbage is tender and slightly caramelized. Season with salt and black pepper to taste. Adjust the seasoning as needed.

Combine the Pasta and Cabbage:
6. Add the cooked and drained egg noodles or pasta to the skillet with the cabbage mixture.
7. Toss everything together to combine, allowing the flavors to meld for a few minutes over low heat.

Serve your Krautfleckerl:
8. Spoon the cabbage pasta onto serving plates.
9. Garnish with chopped fresh parsley, if desired.
10. Serve with a dollop of sour cream on the side, if you like.

SIDE DISHES AND SALADS

Erdäpfelsalat (Potato Salad)

Servings: 4-6
Preparation Time: 20 minutes
Cooking Time: 15 minutes
Ingredients:
For the Potato Salad:
- 2 pounds (about 4-5 large) russet potatoes, peeled and cut into 1-inch cubes
- 1 small red onion, finely chopped
- 2 tablespoons fresh chives, chopped
- 2 tablespoons fresh parsley, chopped
- Salt and black pepper, to taste

For the Dressing:
- 1/2 cup vegetable oil
- 1/4 cup white wine vinegar
- 1 tablespoon Dijon mustard
- 1 teaspoon granulated sugar
- 2 cloves garlic, minced
- 1/2 teaspoon celery seeds (optional)
- Salt and black pepper, to taste

Instructions:
Boil the Potatoes:
1. Place the peeled and cubed potatoes in a large pot of salted water.

2. Bring the water to a boil, then reduce the heat to a simmer. Cook the potatoes for about 10-12 minutes or until they are fork-tender but not falling apart.
3. Drain the cooked potatoes and let them cool to room temperature.

Prepare the Dressing:

4. In a small bowl, whisk together the vegetable oil, white wine vinegar, Dijon mustard, granulated sugar, minced garlic, and celery seeds (if using). Season with salt and black pepper to taste. Adjust the seasoning as needed.

Assemble the Potato Salad:

5. Place the cooled potatoes in a large mixing bowl.
6. Add the finely chopped red onion, fresh chives, and fresh parsley to the bowl.
7. Pour the dressing over the potato mixture.
8. Gently toss everything together until the potatoes are well coated with the dressing and the ingredients are evenly distributed.
9. Cover the bowl and refrigerate the potato salad for at least 1 hour before serving to allow the flavors to meld.

Serve your Erdäpfelsalat:

10. Give the potato salad a final toss before serving.
11. Garnish with extra fresh herbs if desired.

Krautsalat (Coleslaw)

Servings: 4-6
Preparation Time: 15 minutes
Ingredients:
For the Coleslaw:
- 1 small green cabbage, thinly sliced or shredded
- 1 carrot, grated
- 1 small red onion, thinly sliced (optional)
- 2 tablespoons fresh parsley, chopped (for garnish, optional)

For the Dressing:
- 1/2 cup mayonnaise
- 2 tablespoons white wine vinegar
- 1 tablespoon granulated sugar
- 1 teaspoon Dijon mustard
- Salt and black pepper, to taste
- 1/2 teaspoon celery seeds (optional)

Instructions:
Prepare the Coleslaw:
1. In a large mixing bowl, combine the thinly sliced or shredded green cabbage, grated carrot, and thinly sliced red onion (if using).

Prepare the Dressing:
2. In a separate bowl, whisk together the mayonnaise, white wine vinegar, granulated sugar, Dijon mustard, and celery seeds (if using). Season with salt and black pepper to taste. Adjust the seasoning as needed.

Combine the Coleslaw:
3. Pour the dressing over the cabbage mixture.
4. Toss everything together until the vegetables are well coated with the dressing and the ingredients are evenly distributed.

Chill and Serve your Krautsalat:
5. Cover the bowl and refrigerate the coleslaw for at least 1 hour before serving to allow the flavors to meld.
6. Give the coleslaw a final toss before serving.

Garnish your Krautsalat:
7. Garnish with chopped fresh parsley, if desired.

Gurkensalat (Cucumber Salad)

Servings: 4-6
Preparation Time: 15 minutes
Ingredients:
For the Cucumber Salad:
- 4 medium cucumbers, thinly sliced
- 1 small red onion, thinly sliced
- 2 tablespoons fresh dill, chopped (for garnish, optional)

For the Dressing:
- 1/2 cup sour cream
- 2 tablespoons white wine vinegar
- 1 tablespoon granulated sugar
- Salt and black pepper, to taste

Instructions:
Prepare the Cucumber Salad:
1. In a large mixing bowl, combine the thinly sliced cucumbers and thinly sliced red onion.

Prepare the Dressing:

2. In a separate bowl, whisk together the sour cream, white wine vinegar, granulated sugar, salt, and black pepper to taste. Adjust the seasoning as needed.

Combine the Cucumber Salad:
3. Pour the dressing over the cucumber and onion mixture.
4. Toss everything together until the vegetables are well coated with the dressing and the ingredients are evenly distributed.

Chill and Serve your Gurkensalat:
5. Cover the bowl and refrigerate the cucumber salad for at least 30 minutes before serving to allow the flavors to meld.
6. Give the salad a final toss before serving.

Garnish your Gurkensalat:
7. Garnish with chopped fresh dill, if desired.

Rösti (Swiss Potato Pancakes)

Servings: 4
Preparation Time: 20 minutes
Cooking Time: 30 minutes
Ingredients:
- 4 large russet potatoes, peeled and grated
- 2 tablespoons butter
- 2 tablespoons vegetable oil
- Salt and black pepper, to taste

Instructions:

Prepare the Grated Potatoes:
1. Peel the russet potatoes and grate them using a coarse grater. Place the grated potatoes in a clean kitchen towel and squeeze out as much moisture as possible.

Cook the Rösti:
2. In a large non-stick skillet, heat the butter and vegetable oil over medium-high heat.
3. Add the grated potatoes to the skillet, spreading them out evenly to form a large pancake shape.
4. Season the top of the potato pancake with salt and black pepper to taste.
5. Cook the potato pancake for about 10-15 minutes on medium-high heat, or until the bottom is golden brown and crisp.
6. Carefully flip the potato pancake over. You can do this by sliding it onto a large plate, then placing the skillet upside down over the

plate and quickly inverting it. Alternatively, use a spatula to flip the pancake if you're comfortable with it.
7. Continue to cook for another 10-15 minutes, or until the other side is golden brown and the potatoes are cooked through and tender.
8. Slide the rösti onto a serving plate.

Serve your Rösti:
9. Cut the rösti into wedges or slices and serve hot.

Semmelknödel (Bread Dumplings)

Servings: 4-6
Preparation Time: 20 minutes
Cooking Time: 20 minutes
Ingredients:
- 6 stale rolls or 1 large loaf of stale bread
- 1 cup milk
- 2 large eggs
- 1 small onion, finely chopped
- 2 tablespoons butter
- 2 tablespoons fresh parsley, chopped
- Salt and black pepper, to taste
- 1/2 teaspoon ground nutmeg (optional)

Instructions:
Prepare the Bread:
1. Cut the stale rolls or bread into small cubes or tear them into small pieces. Place them in a large mixing bowl.
2. Heat the milk until it's hot but not boiling. Pour the hot milk over the bread cubes. Let them soak for about 10 minutes, or until they absorb the milk and become soft.

Sauté the Onion:
3. In a skillet, melt the butter over medium heat.
4. Add the finely chopped onion and sauté for about 3-4 minutes until the onion becomes translucent and fragrant.

Prepare the Dumpling Mixture:
5. In the bowl with the soaked bread, add the sautéed onions, chopped fresh parsley, large eggs, salt, black pepper, and ground nutmeg (if using).
6. Use your hands or a wooden spoon to thoroughly mix and knead the dumpling mixture until it's well combined. If the mixture is

too wet, you can add a bit more bread or breadcrumbs to achieve the desired consistency.
Shape and Cook the Dumplings:
7. Divide the dumpling mixture into 6 equal portions.
8. With wet hands, shape each portion into a round dumpling, about the size of a tennis ball.
9. Bring a large pot of salted water to a boil.
10. Carefully lower the dumplings into the boiling water. Reduce the heat to low and let them simmer for about 15-20 minutes, or until they float to the surface and are cooked through. Be gentle when handling the dumplings to prevent them from falling apart.

Serve your Semmelknödel:
11. Using a slotted spoon, remove the cooked dumplings from the water and drain them briefly.
12. Serve the Semmelknödel hot as a delightful side dish for roasted meats, stews, or mushroom sauces.

Rote Rüben Salat (Beetroot Salad)

Servings: 4-6
Preparation Time: 15 minutes
Cooking Time: 40 minutes (for roasting the beets)
Ingredients:
For the Salad:
- 4 medium-sized beetroots (red beets), trimmed and washed
- 1 small red onion, thinly sliced
- 1/2 cup walnuts, toasted and roughly chopped
- 2 tablespoons fresh parsley, chopped (for garnish, optional)

For the Dressing:
- 1/4 cup olive oil
- 2 tablespoons white wine vinegar
- 1 teaspoon Dijon mustard
- 1 teaspoon honey or maple syrup (optional, for sweetness)
- Salt and black pepper, to taste

Instructions:
Roast the Beetroots:
1. Preheat your oven to 400°F (200°C).
2. Wrap each beetroot individually in aluminum foil. Place them on a baking sheet.
3. Roast the beets in the preheated oven for about 40 minutes, or

until they are tender when pierced with a fork. The cooking time may vary depending on the size of the beets.
4. Remove the roasted beets from the oven and let them cool for a few minutes. Then, peel and thinly slice them.

Prepare the Dressing:
5. In a small bowl, whisk together the olive oil, white wine vinegar, Dijon mustard, honey or maple syrup (if using), salt, and black pepper. Adjust the seasoning to your taste.

Assemble the Beetroot Salad:
6. In a large serving bowl, combine the sliced roasted beets and thinly sliced red onion.
7. Drizzle the dressing over the beet and onion mixture.
8. Toss everything together gently to coat the vegetables with the dressing.

Serve your Rote Rüben Salat:
9. Sprinkle the toasted and chopped walnuts over the salad.
10. Garnish with chopped fresh parsley, if desired.

Kartoffelgratin (Potato Gratin)

Servings: 4-6
Preparation Time: 20 minutes
Cooking Time: 1 hour
Ingredients:

- 2 pounds (about 4-5 large) russet potatoes, peeled and thinly sliced
- 2 cups heavy cream
- 2 cloves garlic, minced
- 2 cups grated Gruyère cheese (or any Swiss cheese)
- 2 tablespoons unsalted butter
- Salt and black pepper, to taste
- Fresh thyme leaves, for garnish (optional)

Instructions:

Prepare the Potatoes:
1. Preheat your oven to 375°F (190°C).
2. Peel the russet potatoes and thinly slice them into rounds. You can use a mandoline slicer for even slices if available.

Prepare the Cream Mixture:
3. In a saucepan over medium heat, combine the heavy cream and minced garlic. Heat the mixture until it's warm but not boiling.

Remove it from the heat.

Layer the Potato Gratin:
4. Grease a large ovenproof baking dish with butter.
5. Arrange a layer of the thinly sliced potatoes in the bottom of the baking dish, slightly overlapping them.
6. Sprinkle a portion of the grated Gruyère cheese over the potatoes.
7. Season the layer with salt and black pepper to taste.
8. Repeat the process, creating additional layers of potatoes, cheese, and seasoning until you've used all the potatoes.

Pour the Cream Mixture:
9. Pour the warm garlic-infused heavy cream evenly over the layers of potatoes and cheese.

Bake the Potato Gratin:
10. Cover the baking dish with aluminum foil.
11. Bake in the preheated oven for about 45 minutes.
12. Remove the foil and continue to bake for an additional 15-20 minutes, or until the top is golden brown and the potatoes are tender when pierced with a knife.

Serve your Kartoffelgratin:
13. Let the potato gratin cool for a few minutes before serving.
14. Garnish with fresh thyme leaves, if desired.

Rahmspinat (Creamed Spinach)

Servings: 4
Preparation Time: 10 minutes
Cooking Time: 15 minutes
Ingredients:
- 1 pound fresh spinach leaves, washed and trimmed
- 2 tablespoons butter
- 2 cloves garlic, minced
- 1/2 cup heavy cream
- 1/4 cup grated Parmesan cheese
- Salt and black pepper, to taste
- A pinch of ground nutmeg (optional)

Instructions:

Prepare the Spinach:
1. Wash the fresh spinach leaves thoroughly and remove any tough stems or damaged leaves. Drain well.

Cook the Rahmspinat:
2. In a large skillet, melt the butter over medium heat.
3. Add the minced garlic and sauté for about 1-2 minutes until fragrant but not browned.
4. Add the washed and trimmed spinach leaves to the skillet. You may need to add the spinach in batches, allowing it to wilt down as it cooks.
5. Cook the spinach for about 3-5 minutes, or until it's fully wilted and tender. Stir occasionally.
6. Pour in the heavy cream and grated Parmesan cheese. Stir well to combine.
7. Season the creamed spinach with salt, black pepper, and a pinch of ground nutmeg (if using). Adjust the seasoning to your taste.
8. Continue to cook for an additional 3-5 minutes, allowing the cream to thicken and the flavors to meld.

Serve your Rahmspinat:
9. Transfer the creamed spinach to a serving dish.

Karottensalat (Carrot Salad)

Servings: 4-6
Preparation Time: 15 minutes
Ingredients:
For the Carrot Salad:
- 4-5 large carrots, peeled and coarsely grated
- 1/4 cup raisins
- 1/4 cup chopped walnuts
- 2 tablespoons fresh parsley, chopped (for garnish, optional)

For the Dressing:
- 3 tablespoons olive oil
- 2 tablespoons white wine vinegar
- 1 tablespoon honey
- 1 teaspoon Dijon mustard
- Salt and black pepper, to taste

Instructions:
Prepare the Carrot Salad:
1. Peel the large carrots and coarsely grate them using a box grater or a food processor.
2. In a large mixing bowl, combine the coarsely grated carrots, raisins, and chopped walnuts.

Prepare the Dressing:
3. In a small bowl, whisk together the olive oil, white wine vinegar, honey, Dijon mustard, salt, and black pepper to taste. Adjust the seasoning as needed.

Combine the Carrot Salad:
4. Pour the dressing over the carrot, raisin, and walnut mixture.
5. Toss everything together until the carrots are well coated with the dressing and the ingredients are evenly distributed.

Chill and Serve your Karottensalat:
6. Cover the bowl and refrigerate the carrot salad for at least 30 minutes before serving to allow the flavors to meld.
7. Give the salad a final toss before serving.

Garnish your Karottensalat:
8. Garnish with chopped fresh parsley, if desired.

Kartoffelsalat (Warm Potato Salad)

Servings: 4-6
Preparation Time: 15 minutes
Cooking Time: 20 minutes
Ingredients:

For the Warm Potato Salad:
- 2 pounds (about 4-5 large) russet potatoes, peeled and cut into 1-inch cubes
- 1 small red onion, finely chopped
- 2 tablespoons fresh chives, chopped
- 2 tablespoons fresh parsley, chopped
- 4 slices bacon, cooked and crumbled (optional)
- Salt and black pepper, to taste

For the Dressing:
- 1/4 cup vegetable or olive oil
- 3 tablespoons white wine vinegar
- 1 teaspoon Dijon mustard
- 1 teaspoon granulated sugar
- 2 cloves garlic, minced
- Salt and black pepper, to taste

Instructions:
Boil the Potatoes:
1. Place the peeled and cubed potatoes in a large pot of salted water.
2. Bring the water to a boil, then reduce the heat to a simmer. Cook

the potatoes for about 10-12 minutes or until they are fork-tender but not falling apart.
3. Drain the cooked potatoes and let them cool slightly.

Prepare the Dressing:
4. In a small bowl, whisk together the vegetable or olive oil, white wine vinegar, Dijon mustard, granulated sugar, minced garlic, salt, and black pepper to taste. Adjust the seasoning as needed.

Assemble the Warm Potato Salad:
5. While the potatoes are still warm, transfer them to a large mixing bowl.
6. Add the finely chopped red onion, fresh chives, and fresh parsley to the bowl.
7. Pour the dressing over the warm potato mixture.
8. Toss everything together gently until the potatoes are well coated with the dressing and the ingredients are evenly distributed.
9. If using, sprinkle the crumbled bacon over the top.

Serve your Kartoffelsalat:
10. Serve the warm potato salad immediately as a comforting side dish or as a delicious accompaniment to grilled meats.

DESSERTS AND PASTRIES

Sachertorte

Servings: 12
Preparation Time: 30 minutes
Baking Time: 40 minutes
Ingredients:
For the Cake:
- 1 cup (225 grams) unsalted butter, softened
- 1 cup (200 grams) granulated sugar
- 7 large eggs, separated
- 1 teaspoon vanilla extract
- 7 ounces (200 grams) dark chocolate, melted and cooled
- 1 1/2 cups (180 grams) all-purpose flour
- 1/4 cup (25 grams) cocoa powder
- 1/2 teaspoon baking powder
- Pinch of salt

For the Apricot Jam Filling:
- 1 cup apricot jam

For the Chocolate Glaze:
- 7 ounces (200 grams) dark chocolate, chopped
- 1/2 cup (120 milliliters) heavy cream
- 2 tablespoons unsalted butter

Instructions:
Prepare the Cake:

1. Preheat your oven to 350°F (180°C). Grease and flour a 9-inch (23-centimeter) round cake pan.
2. In a large mixing bowl, cream together the softened butter and granulated sugar until light and fluffy.
3. Add the egg yolks one at a time, mixing well after each addition. Stir in the vanilla extract.
4. Mix in the melted and cooled dark chocolate until well combined.
5. In a separate bowl, sift together the all-purpose flour, cocoa powder, baking powder, and a pinch of salt.
6. Gradually add the dry ingredients to the chocolate mixture, mixing until just combined.
7. In another clean bowl, whip the egg whites until stiff peaks form.
8. Gently fold the whipped egg whites into the chocolate batter, being careful not to deflate the egg whites.
9. Pour the batter into the prepared cake pan and smooth the top.
10. Bake in the preheated oven for about 40 minutes or until a toothpick inserted into the center comes out clean.
11. Remove the cake from the oven and let it cool in the pan for 10 minutes before transferring it to a wire rack to cool completely.

Assemble the Sachertorte:

12. Once the cake has cooled, slice it horizontally into two equal layers.
13. Heat the apricot jam in a small saucepan until it becomes smooth and spreadable. Then, spread a layer of the jam on the bottom cake layer.
14. Place the second cake layer on top of the jam and press gently to adhere.

Prepare the Chocolate Glaze:

15. In a heatproof bowl, combine the chopped dark chocolate, heavy cream, and unsalted butter.
16. Place the bowl over a pot of simmering water (double boiler) and stir until the chocolate and butter have melted and the mixture is smooth.

Finish the Sachertorte:

17. Pour the warm chocolate glaze over the top of the cake, allowing it to flow down the sides and cover the cake evenly.
18. Let the glaze set for a few hours at room temperature.
19. Before serving, you can decorate the top of the Sachertorte with a chocolate "Sacher" inscription or simply dust it with cocoa

powder.

Apfelstrudel (Apple Strudel)

Servings: 8-10
Preparation Time: 30 minutes
Baking Time: 45 minutes
Ingredients:
For the Strudel Dough:
- 2 cups (250 grams) all-purpose flour
- 1/2 teaspoon salt
- 2 tablespoons vegetable oil
- 3/4 cup lukewarm water

For the Filling:
- 6-8 medium apples (such as Granny Smith or Braeburn), peeled, cored, and thinly sliced
- 1 cup breadcrumbs
- 1 cup granulated sugar
- 1 1/2 teaspoons ground cinnamon
- 1/2 cup raisins (optional)
- Zest of 1 lemon
- Juice of 1 lemon
- 1/2 cup melted unsalted butter, for brushing

For Dusting and Garnish:
- Powdered sugar, for dusting
- Whipped cream or vanilla ice cream (optional)

Instructions:
Prepare the Strudel Dough:
1. In a large mixing bowl, combine the all-purpose flour and salt.
2. Make a well in the center of the flour mixture and add the vegetable oil and lukewarm water.
3. Mix the ingredients together until a dough forms. Knead the dough on a floured surface until it becomes smooth and elastic. Form it into a ball.
4. Brush the dough with a little vegetable oil, place it back in the bowl, cover it with a clean kitchen towel, and let it rest for about 30 minutes.

Prepare the Filling:
5. In a separate bowl, combine the thinly sliced apples, breadcrumbs, granulated sugar, ground cinnamon, raisins (if

using), lemon zest, and lemon juice. Toss everything together until the apples are well coated.

Assemble the Apfelstrudel:
6. Preheat your oven to 350°F (180°C). Line a baking sheet with parchment paper.
7. Roll out the rested strudel dough on a floured surface into a large, thin rectangle. You can use a rolling pin or gently stretch the dough with your hands to achieve the desired thinness.
8. Brush the entire surface of the dough with the melted unsalted butter.
9. Pile the apple filling onto one long side of the dough, leaving about 2 inches of dough free on each short end.
10. Fold in the short ends of the dough over the filling.
11. Carefully roll up the dough, starting from the long side with the filling. Use the parchment paper to help you lift and roll the strudel.

Bake the Apfelstrudel:
12. Place the rolled strudel, seam-side down, on the prepared baking sheet.
13. Brush the top of the strudel with a bit more melted butter.
14. Bake in the preheated oven for about 45 minutes, or until the strudel is golden brown and the apples are tender.

Serve your Apfelstrudel:
15. Let the strudel cool slightly before dusting it generously with powdered sugar.
16. Slice and serve your Apfelstrudel warm, either on its own or with a dollop of whipped cream or a scoop of vanilla ice cream.

Linzer Torte

Servings: 8-10
Preparation Time: 30 minutes
Baking Time: 35-40 minutes
Ingredients:
For the Dough:
- 2 cups (250 grams) all-purpose flour
- 1 cup (225 grams) unsalted butter, cold and cubed
- 1/2 cup (100 grams) granulated sugar
- 1 1/4 cups (150 grams) ground almonds or hazelnuts
- 1 teaspoon ground cinnamon

- 1/2 teaspoon lemon zest
- 1 large egg
- 1/4 teaspoon salt

For the Filling:
- 1 1/2 cups raspberry jam (or any berry jam of your choice)
- 1/2 cup ground almonds or hazelnuts, for sprinkling
- Powdered sugar, for dusting

Instructions:

Prepare the Linzer Torte Dough:
1. In a food processor, combine the all-purpose flour, cold and cubed unsalted butter, granulated sugar, ground almonds or hazelnuts, ground cinnamon, lemon zest, egg, and salt.
2. Pulse the ingredients together until they form a crumbly texture.
3. Turn the mixture out onto a clean surface and knead it briefly until it comes together into a smooth dough. Form the dough into a disk, wrap it in plastic wrap, and refrigerate for at least 30 minutes.

Assemble the Linzer Torte:
4. Preheat your oven to 350°F (180°C). Grease and flour a 9-inch (23-centimeter) tart pan with a removable bottom.
5. Take 2/3 of the chilled dough and roll it out on a floured surface to fit the bottom of the tart pan. Carefully press the dough into the bottom of the pan.
6. Spread a thin layer of ground almonds or hazelnuts over the dough. This helps absorb any excess moisture from the jam.
7. Evenly spread the raspberry jam (or your preferred berry jam) over the nut layer.
8. Roll out the remaining 1/3 of the dough into long strips, about 1/4-inch thick.
9. Create a lattice pattern on top of the jam by arranging the strips in a crisscross fashion.

Bake the Linzer Torte:
10. Place the tart pan on a baking sheet (to catch any potential drips) and bake in the preheated oven for about 35-40 minutes, or until the edges of the tart are golden brown and the jam is bubbling.

Finish your Linzer Torte:
11. Remove the tart from the oven and let it cool in the pan for a while.
12. Once the tart has cooled to room temperature, carefully remove

it from the tart pan.
13. Dust the Linzer Torte with powdered sugar for a beautiful finish.
Serve your Linzer Torte:
14. Slice and serve your Linzer Torte as a classic Austrian dessert, perfect with a cup of tea or coffee.

Topfenstrudel (Quark Strudel)

Servings: 8-10
Preparation Time: 30 minutes
Baking Time: 35-40 minutes
Ingredients:
For the Strudel Dough:
- 2 cups (250 grams) all-purpose flour
- 1/4 cup (60 milliliters) vegetable oil
- 1/2 teaspoon salt
- 1/2 cup lukewarm water
- 1 large egg, beaten (for brushing)

For the Quark Filling:
- 2 cups (500 grams) quark cheese (or substitute with farmer's cheese or ricotta)
- 1/2 cup (100 grams) granulated sugar
- 2 large eggs
- 2 tablespoons unsalted butter, melted
- 1 teaspoon vanilla extract
- Zest of 1 lemon
- 1/4 cup (30 grams) semolina or fine breadcrumbs
- 1/4 cup (60 milliliters) heavy cream

For Dusting and Garnish:
- Powdered sugar, for dusting
- Fresh berries or berry sauce (optional)

Instructions:
Prepare the Strudel Dough:
1. In a large mixing bowl, combine the all-purpose flour and salt.
2. Make a well in the center of the flour mixture and add the vegetable oil and lukewarm water.
3. Mix the ingredients together until a dough forms. Knead the dough on a floured surface until it becomes smooth and elastic. Form it into a ball.
4. Brush the dough with a little vegetable oil, place it back in the

bowl, cover it with a clean kitchen towel, and let it rest for about 30 minutes.

Prepare the Quark Filling:

5. In a mixing bowl, combine the quark cheese, granulated sugar, eggs, melted unsalted butter, vanilla extract, lemon zest, semolina or fine breadcrumbs, and heavy cream. Mix everything together until well combined.

Assemble the Topfenstrudel:

6. Preheat your oven to 350°F (180°C). Line a baking sheet with parchment paper.
7. Roll out the rested strudel dough on a floured surface into a large, thin rectangle. You can use a rolling pin or gently stretch the dough with your hands to achieve the desired thinness.
8. Brush the entire surface of the dough with the beaten egg.
9. Spread the prepared quark filling evenly over the dough, leaving a border around the edges.
10. Carefully fold in the short ends of the dough over the filling.
11. Roll up the dough, starting from the long side with the filling. Use the parchment paper to help you lift and roll the strudel.
12. Transfer the strudel, seam-side down, to the prepared baking sheet.

Bake the Topfenstrudel:

13. Brush the top of the strudel with a bit more beaten egg.
14. Bake in the preheated oven for about 35-40 minutes, or until the strudel is golden brown and the filling is set.

Finish your Topfenstrudel:

15. Remove the strudel from the oven and let it cool slightly.
16. Dust the Topfenstrudel with powdered sugar for a beautiful finish.

Serve your Topfenstrudel:

17. Slice and serve your Topfenstrudel warm, either on its own or with a drizzle of berry sauce or a handful of fresh berries.

Esterházy Torte

Servings: 12
Preparation Time: 1 hour
Baking Time: 30-35 minutes
Ingredients:
For the Cake:

- 1 cup (225 grams) unsalted butter, softened
- 1 cup (200 grams) granulated sugar
- 6 large eggs, separated
- 2 cups (200 grams) ground almonds or hazelnuts
- 1 cup (120 grams) all-purpose flour
- 1 teaspoon baking powder
- 1/2 teaspoon salt
- 1 teaspoon vanilla extract

For the Buttercream:
- 1 1/4 cups (280 grams) unsalted butter, softened
- 1 1/2 cups (180 grams) powdered sugar
- 1 teaspoon vanilla extract
- 3 tablespoons dark rum (optional)
- 1/4 cup (25 grams) cocoa powder

For the Glaze:
- 1/2 cup (120 milliliters) water
- 1/2 cup (100 grams) granulated sugar
- 1/4 cup (60 grams) apricot jam
- 3.5 ounces (100 grams) dark chocolate, chopped
- 1 tablespoon unsalted butter

Instructions:

Prepare the Cake:

1. Preheat your oven to 350°F (180°C). Grease and flour two 9-inch (23-centimeter) round cake pans.
2. In a large mixing bowl, cream together the softened butter and granulated sugar until light and fluffy.
3. Add the egg yolks one at a time, mixing well after each addition. Stir in the vanilla extract.
4. In a separate bowl, combine the ground almonds or hazelnuts, all-purpose flour, baking powder, and salt.
5. Gradually add the dry ingredients to the butter mixture and mix until just combined.
6. In another clean bowl, whip the egg whites until stiff peaks form.
7. Gently fold the whipped egg whites into the cake batter until no streaks remain.
8. Divide the batter evenly between the prepared cake pans and smooth the tops.
9. Bake in the preheated oven for about 30-35 minutes, or until a toothpick inserted into the center of the cakes comes out clean.

10. Remove the cakes from the oven and let them cool in the pans for 10 minutes before transferring them to a wire rack to cool completely.

Prepare the Buttercream:
11. In a mixing bowl, beat the softened butter until creamy and smooth.
12. Gradually add the powdered sugar, vanilla extract, and dark rum (if using). Beat until the buttercream is light and fluffy.
13. Divide the buttercream into two equal portions.
14. In one portion of buttercream, sift in the cocoa powder and mix until well combined. This is your chocolate buttercream.

Assemble the Esterházy Torte:
15. Place one of the cooled cake layers on a serving plate.
16. Spread a layer of the plain (non-chocolate) buttercream over the top of the first cake layer.
17. Carefully place the second cake layer on top of the buttercream.
18. Spread the chocolate buttercream evenly over the top of the second cake layer.
19. Using a sharp knife or cake comb, create a decorative pattern on the surface of the chocolate buttercream.

Prepare the Glaze:
20. In a small saucepan, combine the water, granulated sugar, and apricot jam. Bring the mixture to a simmer over medium heat, stirring until the sugar has dissolved.
21. Remove the saucepan from the heat and stir in the chopped dark chocolate and butter until the glaze is smooth and glossy.

Finish your Esterházy Torte:
22. Pour the chocolate glaze over the top of the cake, allowing it to flow down the sides and cover the cake evenly.
23. Let the glaze set for a while.

Kaiserschmarrn

Servings: 4
Preparation Time: 10 minutes
Cooking Time: 15 minutes
Ingredients:
- 2 cups (250 grams) all-purpose flour
- 2 tablespoons granulated sugar
- A pinch of salt

- 4 large eggs, separated
- 1 1/2 cups (360 milliliters) milk
- 2 tablespoons unsalted butter
- 1/2 cup (60 grams) raisins (optional)
- Powdered sugar, for dusting
- Plum or apple compote, for serving (optional)

Instructions:

Prepare the Batter:

1. In a large mixing bowl, whisk together the all-purpose flour, granulated sugar, and a pinch of salt.
2. In a separate bowl, separate the egg yolks from the egg whites.
3. Add the egg yolks and milk to the dry ingredients in the large mixing bowl. Whisk everything together until you have a smooth batter.
4. In another clean bowl, whip the egg whites until stiff peaks form.
5. Gently fold the whipped egg whites into the batter until well combined. Be careful not to deflate the egg whites.

Cook the Kaiserschmarrn:

6. In a large, ovenproof skillet, melt the unsalted butter over medium-high heat.
7. Pour the batter into the skillet and spread it out evenly. If using, sprinkle the raisins evenly over the batter.
8. Cook the Kaiserschmarrn for about 5-7 minutes or until the edges start to set and become golden brown.
9. Carefully flip the Kaiserschmarrn over in sections using a spatula or by tearing it apart with two forks. You want to create irregular chunks.
10. Continue to cook for another 5-7 minutes until the other side is golden brown and the inside is cooked through but still soft and slightly gooey.

Serve your Kaiserschmarrn:

11. Remove the skillet from the heat and dust the Kaiserschmarrn generously with powdered sugar.
12. You can serve Kaiserschmarrn on its own or with a dollop of plum or apple compote for extra flavor.

Palatschinken (Austrian Pancakes)

Servings: 4
Preparation Time: 10 minutes

Cooking Time: 20 minutes
Ingredients:
For the Pancake Batter:
- 1 cup (125 grams) all-purpose flour
- 1 tablespoon granulated sugar
- A pinch of salt
- 2 large eggs
- 1 1/4 cups (300 milliliters) milk
- 2 tablespoons unsalted butter, melted
- 1/2 teaspoon vanilla extract

For Filling and Topping:
- Apricot jam or fruit preserves
- Powdered sugar, for dusting
- Whipped cream (optional)

Instructions:
Prepare the Pancake Batter:
1. In a large mixing bowl, combine the all-purpose flour, granulated sugar, and a pinch of salt.
2. In a separate bowl, whisk together the eggs, milk, melted unsalted butter, and vanilla extract until well combined.
3. Gradually pour the wet ingredients into the dry ingredients while whisking continuously until you have a smooth batter. Let the batter rest for about 10 minutes.

Cook the Palatschinken:
4. Heat a non-stick skillet or crepe pan over medium heat. Add a small amount of butter or oil and swirl it around to coat the bottom of the pan evenly.
5. Pour a ladleful of the pancake batter into the hot skillet, tilting the pan to spread the batter evenly and create a thin pancake.
6. Cook the pancake for about 1-2 minutes on one side until it's lightly golden. Flip it over using a spatula and cook for another 1-2 minutes on the other side until both sides are golden.
7. Transfer the cooked Palatschinken to a plate and repeat the process with the remaining batter. You can stack the cooked pancakes on top of each other.

Fill and Serve your Palatschinken:
8. Once all the pancakes are cooked, spread a thin layer of apricot jam or fruit preserves on each pancake.
9. Roll up the pancakes into a cylinder or fold them into quarters.

Finish your Palatschinken:
10. Dust the Palatschinken with powdered sugar.
11. If desired, serve with a dollop of whipped cream.

Mohr im Hemd (Chocolate Pudding)

Servings: 6-8
Preparation Time: 20 minutes
Cooking Time: 30 minutes
Ingredients:
For the Chocolate Pudding:
- 4 ounces (115 grams) semisweet chocolate, chopped
- 1/2 cup (115 grams) unsalted butter
- 3/4 cup (150 grams) granulated sugar
- 3 large eggs, separated
- 1 teaspoon vanilla extract
- 1 cup (100 grams) ground almonds or hazelnuts
- 2 tablespoons all-purpose flour
- A pinch of salt

For the Chocolate Glaze:
- 4 ounces (115 grams) semisweet chocolate, chopped
- 1/4 cup (60 milliliters) heavy cream
- 1 tablespoon unsalted butter

For Serving:
- Whipped cream (optional)
- A sprinkle of cocoa powder (optional)

Instructions:
Prepare the Chocolate Pudding:
1. Preheat your oven to 350°F (180°C). Grease and flour individual ramekins or a baking dish that can accommodate all the pudding.
2. In a heatproof bowl, combine the chopped semisweet chocolate and unsalted butter. Place the bowl over a pot of simmering water (double boiler) and stir until the chocolate and butter have melted and the mixture is smooth. Remove it from the heat and let it cool slightly.
3. In a separate mixing bowl, beat the egg yolks and granulated sugar together until pale and fluffy. Stir in the vanilla extract.
4. Gradually mix the melted chocolate and butter mixture into the egg yolk and sugar mixture.
5. Add the ground almonds or hazelnuts, all-purpose flour, and a

pinch of salt to the chocolate mixture. Stir until well combined.
6. In another clean bowl, whip the egg whites until stiff peaks form.
7. Gently fold the whipped egg whites into the chocolate mixture until no streaks remain.

Bake the Chocolate Pudding:
8. Pour the chocolate pudding mixture into the prepared ramekins or baking dish.
9. Bake in the preheated oven for about 25-30 minutes, or until the pudding is set and a toothpick inserted into the center comes out with a few moist crumbs.

Prepare the Chocolate Glaze:
10. While the pudding is baking, prepare the chocolate glaze. In a saucepan, combine the chopped semisweet chocolate, heavy cream, and unsalted butter. Heat over low heat, stirring continuously, until the mixture is smooth and glossy. Remove from heat and set aside.

Finish your Mohr im Hemd:
11. Once the pudding is done baking, remove it from the oven and let it cool slightly.
12. Pour the warm chocolate glaze over the top of the pudding, allowing it to flow down the sides.

Serve your Mohr im Hemd:
13. Optionally, serve your Mohr im Hemd with a dollop of whipped cream and a sprinkle of cocoa powder.

Marillenknödel (Apricot Dumplings)

Servings: 4-6
Preparation Time: 30 minutes
Cooking Time: 15 minutes
Ingredients:
For the Dumplings:
- 6 large apricots, ripe but firm
- 1 1/2 cups (180 grams) all-purpose flour
- A pinch of salt
- 2 tablespoons granulated sugar
- 2 large eggs
- 2 tablespoons unsalted butter, melted

For the Coating:
- 1/2 cup (60 grams) breadcrumbs

- 2 tablespoons unsalted butter
- 2 tablespoons granulated sugar
- 1 teaspoon ground cinnamon

For Serving:
- Powdered sugar, for dusting
- Whipped cream (optional)

Instructions:

Prepare the Apricot Dumplings:
1. Wash the apricots and cut them in half. Remove the pits and set the apricot halves aside.
2. In a mixing bowl, combine the all-purpose flour, a pinch of salt, and 2 tablespoons of granulated sugar.
3. Add the eggs and melted unsalted butter to the dry ingredients. Mix until a soft dough forms.
4. Take a small portion of the dough and flatten it in your hand. Place an apricot half in the center and wrap the dough around it, forming a smooth ball. Ensure the apricot is completely enclosed.
5. Repeat this process for all the apricot halves, forming the dumplings.

Cook the Apricot Dumplings:
6. In a large pot, bring water to a gentle boil. Add a pinch of salt to the boiling water.
7. Carefully place the apricot dumplings into the simmering water. Cook them for about 10-12 minutes, or until they float to the surface. Use a slotted spoon to remove them from the water.

Prepare the Coating:
8. In a skillet, melt 2 tablespoons of unsalted butter over medium heat.
9. Add the breadcrumbs to the melted butter and stir continuously until the breadcrumbs turn golden brown. This should take about 5 minutes.
10. Remove the skillet from heat and stir in 2 tablespoons of granulated sugar and 1 teaspoon of ground cinnamon. Mix well.

Finish your Marillenknödel:
11. Roll the cooked apricot dumplings in the breadcrumb mixture until they are evenly coated.

Serve your Marillenknödel:
12. Dust the Marillenknödel with powdered sugar and optionally serve them with a dollop of whipped cream.

Mohnnudeln (Poppy Seed Noodles)

Servings: 4-6
Preparation Time: 20 minutes
Cooking Time: 15 minutes
Ingredients:
For the Noodles:
- 10.5 ounces (300 grams) egg noodles or wide egg pasta
- 1/2 cup (120 grams) unsalted butter
- 1/2 cup (60 grams) powdered sugar
- 1 cup (100 grams) ground poppy seeds
- A pinch of salt
- 1/2 teaspoon vanilla extract
- Zest of 1 lemon
- 1/4 cup (60 milliliters) heavy cream
- 1/4 cup (60 milliliters) milk

For Serving:
- Additional powdered sugar, for dusting

Instructions:
Prepare the Noodles:
1. Cook the egg noodles or wide egg pasta according to the package instructions until they are al dente. Drain and set them aside.

Prepare the Poppy Seed Mixture:
2. In a skillet, melt the unsalted butter over medium heat.
3. Add the powdered sugar, ground poppy seeds, a pinch of salt, vanilla extract, and lemon zest to the melted butter. Stir well to combine.
4. Pour in the heavy cream and milk, and continue to cook the mixture over low heat, stirring constantly. Cook for about 5 minutes until the mixture thickens slightly and becomes creamy. Remove it from heat.

Combine the Noodles and Poppy Seed Mixture:
5. Add the cooked noodles to the skillet with the poppy seed mixture.
6. Gently toss the noodles to coat them evenly with the poppy seed mixture. Be careful not to break the noodles.

Serve your Mohnnudeln:
7. Transfer the Mohnnudeln to serving plates.
8. Dust the Mohnnudeln generously with powdered sugar just

before serving.

BREADS AND BAKING

Bauernbrot (Austrian Farm Bread)

Servings: 1 large loaf
Preparation Time: 20 minutes
Baking Time: 45-50 minutes
Ingredients:
For the Bread:
- 4 cups (500 grams) bread flour
- 1 1/2 cups (360 milliliters) lukewarm water
- 2 teaspoons active dry yeast
- 1 teaspoon granulated sugar
- 2 teaspoons salt
- 1 tablespoon vegetable oil

For the Topping (optional):
- Coarse sea salt or flaky salt
- A handful of rolled oats
- A few sunflower seeds or pumpkin seeds

Instructions:
Prepare the Dough:
1. In a small bowl, combine the lukewarm water, active dry yeast, and granulated sugar. Stir gently and let it sit for about 5-10 minutes until it becomes frothy. This indicates that the yeast is active.
2. In a large mixing bowl, combine the bread flour and salt.

3. Make a well in the center of the flour mixture and pour in the yeast mixture and vegetable oil.
4. Gradually mix the ingredients together until a sticky dough forms.
5. Turn the dough out onto a floured surface and knead it for about 8-10 minutes until it becomes smooth and elastic. You can add a little extra flour if it's too sticky, but try not to overdo it.
6. Place the dough in a greased bowl, cover it with a clean kitchen towel or plastic wrap, and let it rise in a warm, draft-free place for about 1 hour, or until it has doubled in size.

Shape and Proof the Loaf:

7. Once the dough has risen, gently punch it down to release any air bubbles.
8. Shape the dough into a round or oval loaf, depending on your preference.
9. Transfer the shaped loaf to a parchment paper-lined baking sheet or a well-floured proofing basket, seam-side down.
10. Cover the loaf with a clean kitchen towel and let it proof for an additional 30-45 minutes. It should puff up slightly.

Preheat the Oven:

11. While the bread is proofing, preheat your oven to 425°F (220°C). If you have a pizza stone or baking stone, place it in the oven while it preheats.

Bake the Bauernbrot:

12. If you're using a pizza stone or baking stone, carefully slide the parchment paper with the loaf onto the hot stone in the oven. If not, simply place the baking sheet in the oven.
13. Optionally, make shallow slashes on the surface of the bread with a sharp knife or razor blade. This allows the bread to expand while baking.
14. If desired, sprinkle the loaf with coarse sea salt or flaky salt, rolled oats, and a few sunflower seeds or pumpkin seeds for added flavor and texture.
15. Bake the bread in the preheated oven for 45-50 minutes or until it's golden brown and sounds hollow when tapped on the bottom.

Cool and Enjoy:

16. Remove the Bauernbrot from the oven and let it cool on a wire rack for at least 30 minutes before slicing.
17. Slice and enjoy your freshly baked Austrian Farm Bread with

butter, cheese, or your favorite spreads.

Kornspitz (Seed Rolls)

Servings: 8 rolls
Preparation Time: 20 minutes
Resting Time: 1 hour
Baking Time: 20-25 minutes
Ingredients:

For the Dough:
- 2 cups (250 grams) bread flour
- 1 1/4 teaspoons active dry yeast
- 1 teaspoon granulated sugar
- 1 teaspoon salt
- 2/3 cup (160 milliliters) lukewarm water
- 1 tablespoon vegetable oil

For the Topping:
- 2 tablespoons mixed seeds (poppy seeds, sesame seeds, sunflower seeds)
- 1 egg, beaten (for egg wash)

Instructions:
Prepare the Dough:
1. In a small bowl, combine the lukewarm water, active dry yeast, and granulated sugar. Stir gently and let it sit for about 5-10 minutes until it becomes frothy. This indicates that the yeast is active.
2. In a large mixing bowl, combine the bread flour and salt.
3. Make a well in the center of the flour mixture and pour in the yeast mixture and vegetable oil.
4. Gradually mix the ingredients together until a dough forms.
5. Turn the dough out onto a floured surface and knead it for about 8-10 minutes until it becomes smooth and elastic. You can add a little extra flour if it's too sticky, but try not to overdo it.
6. Place the dough in a greased bowl, cover it with a clean kitchen towel or plastic wrap, and let it rise in a warm, draft-free place for about 1 hour, or until it has doubled in size.

Shape the Kornspitz:
7. Once the dough has risen, gently punch it down to release any air bubbles.
8. Divide the dough into 8 equal portions.

9. Roll each portion into a ball and then shape it into an elongated roll, tapering the ends slightly. You can flatten the rolls a bit to achieve the traditional Kornspitz shape.
   Preheat the Oven:
10. Preheat your oven to 400°F (200°C). Place a baking sheet or baking stone in the oven to heat.
    Add the Topping:
11. Brush the tops of the Kornspitz rolls with the beaten egg.
12. Sprinkle the mixed seeds over the egg-washed rolls, ensuring they stick to the surface.
    Bake the Kornspitz:
13. Carefully transfer the rolls onto the preheated baking sheet or baking stone.
14. Bake in the preheated oven for 20-25 minutes or until the rolls are golden brown and sound hollow when tapped on the bottom.
    Cool and Enjoy:
15. Remove the Kornspitz from the oven and let them cool on a wire rack for a few minutes.
16. Serve your freshly baked Kornspitz rolls with butter, cheese, cold cuts, or your favorite sandwich fillings.

Semmeln (Vienna Rolls)

Servings: 12 rolls
Preparation Time: 25 minutes
Resting Time: 1 hour 30 minutes
Baking Time: 15-20 minutes
Ingredients:
For the Dough:
- 4 cups (500 grams) bread flour
- 1 1/2 teaspoons active dry yeast
- 2 teaspoons granulated sugar
- 1 1/2 teaspoons salt
- 1 1/4 cups (300 milliliters) lukewarm water
- 2 tablespoons vegetable oil

For the Topping (optional):
- 1 egg yolk
- 1 tablespoon water
- A pinch of salt
- Poppy seeds or sesame seeds for sprinkling

Instructions:
Prepare the Dough:
1. In a small bowl, combine the lukewarm water, active dry yeast, and granulated sugar. Stir gently and let it sit for about 5-10 minutes until it becomes frothy. This indicates that the yeast is active.
2. In a large mixing bowl, combine the bread flour and salt.
3. Make a well in the center of the flour mixture and pour in the yeast mixture and vegetable oil.
4. Gradually mix the ingredients together until a dough forms.
5. Turn the dough out onto a floured surface and knead it for about 8-10 minutes until it becomes smooth and elastic. You can add a little extra flour if it's too sticky, but try not to overdo it.
6. Place the dough in a greased bowl, cover it with a clean kitchen towel or plastic wrap, and let it rise in a warm, draft-free place for about 1 hour or until it has doubled in size.

Shape the Semmeln:
7. Once the dough has risen, gently punch it down to release any air bubbles.
8. Divide the dough into 12 equal portions.
9. Roll each portion into a ball and then flatten it slightly with the palm of your hand to form a roll. You can also shape them into traditional round rolls or oval Vienna-style rolls.

Preheat the Oven:
10. Preheat your oven to 425°F (220°C). Place a baking sheet or baking stone in the oven to heat.

Add the Topping (optional):
11. In a small bowl, whisk together the egg yolk, water, and a pinch of salt to create an egg wash.
12. Brush the tops of the Semmeln with the egg wash.
13. Sprinkle poppy seeds or sesame seeds over the egg-washed rolls for added flavor and texture.

Bake the Semmeln:
14. Carefully transfer the rolls onto the preheated baking sheet or baking stone.
15. Bake in the preheated oven for 15-20 minutes or until the Semmeln are golden brown and sound hollow when tapped on the bottom.

Cool and Enjoy:

16. Remove the Semmeln from the oven and let them cool on a wire rack for a few minutes.
17. Serve your freshly baked Vienna rolls as a side for soups, sandwiches, or as a delightful accompaniment to your favorite meals.

Gugelhupf (Bundt Cake)

Servings: 12
Preparation Time: 20 minutes
Baking Time: 45-55 minutes
Ingredients:
For the Cake:
- 2 1/2 cups (300 grams) all-purpose flour
- 2 teaspoons baking powder
- 1/2 teaspoon salt
- 1 cup (225 grams) unsalted butter, softened
- 1 1/2 cups (300 grams) granulated sugar
- 4 large eggs
- 1 teaspoon vanilla extract
- 1/2 cup (120 milliliters) whole milk

For the Optional Glaze:
- 1 cup (120 grams) powdered sugar
- 2-3 tablespoons milk
- A splash of lemon juice (optional, for flavor)

For Dusting (optional):
- Powdered sugar

Instructions:
Prepare the Cake:
1. Preheat your oven to 350°F (175°C). Grease and flour a Bundt cake pan, ensuring that it's well coated to prevent sticking.
2. In a mixing bowl, whisk together the all-purpose flour, baking powder, and salt. Set this dry mixture aside.
3. In another mixing bowl, cream together the softened unsalted butter and granulated sugar until the mixture is light and fluffy.
4. Add the eggs one at a time, beating well after each addition. Stir in the vanilla extract.
5. Gradually add the dry flour mixture to the wet ingredients, alternating with the whole milk. Begin and end with the dry ingredients, mixing until just combined. Do not overmix.

6. Pour the cake batter into the prepared Bundt cake pan, spreading it evenly.

Bake the Gugelhupf:

7. Place the cake pan in the preheated oven and bake for 45-55 minutes, or until a toothpick inserted into the center of the cake comes out clean.
8. Remove the cake from the oven and let it cool in the pan for about 10 minutes.
9. After 10 minutes, carefully invert the cake onto a wire rack to cool completely.

Prepare the Optional Glaze (if desired):

10. In a small bowl, whisk together the powdered sugar and milk until you have a smooth glaze. You can add a splash of lemon juice for a hint of citrus flavor, if desired.

Finish and Serve your Gugelhupf:

11. Once the cake has cooled, drizzle the glaze over the top of the Gugelhupf.
12. Optionally, dust the cake with powdered sugar for a decorative touch.
13. Slice and serve your Gugelhupf as a delightful dessert or with a cup of coffee or tea.

Buchteln (Sweet Rolls)

Servings: 12 rolls
Preparation Time: 25 minutes
Resting Time: 1 hour 30 minutes
Baking Time: 20-25 minutes
Ingredients:

For the Dough:
- 3 1/2 cups (440 grams) all-purpose flour
- 1/2 cup (100 grams) granulated sugar
- 1 packet (2 1/4 teaspoons) active dry yeast
- A pinch of salt
- 1 cup (240 milliliters) lukewarm milk
- 1/4 cup (60 grams) unsalted butter, melted
- 2 large eggs
- 1 teaspoon vanilla extract
- Zest of 1 lemon (optional)

For the Filling (optional):

- Fruit preserves or jam (apricot or raspberry work well)
- Powdered sugar, for dusting

Instructions:

Prepare the Dough:

1. In a small bowl, combine the lukewarm milk and granulated sugar. Sprinkle the active dry yeast over the mixture and let it sit for about 5-10 minutes until it becomes frothy. This indicates that the yeast is active.
2. In a large mixing bowl, combine the all-purpose flour and a pinch of salt.
3. Make a well in the center of the flour mixture and pour in the yeast mixture, melted unsalted butter, eggs, vanilla extract, and lemon zest (if using).
4. Gradually mix the ingredients together until a sticky dough forms.
5. Turn the dough out onto a floured surface and knead it for about 8-10 minutes until it becomes smooth and elastic. You can add a little extra flour if it's too sticky, but try not to overdo it.
6. Place the dough in a greased bowl, cover it with a clean kitchen towel or plastic wrap, and let it rise in a warm, draft-free place for about 1 hour or until it has doubled in size.

Shape and Fill the Buchteln:

7. Once the dough has risen, gently punch it down to release any air bubbles.
8. Divide the dough into 12 equal portions.
9. Take each portion of dough and flatten it in your hand. Place a small spoonful of fruit preserves or jam in the center, then seal the dough around the filling, forming a smooth ball. Ensure the filling is completely enclosed.

Preheat the Oven:

10. Preheat your oven to 350°F (175°C). Grease a baking dish or cake pan.

Arrange and Bake the Buchteln:

11. Place the filled dough balls in the greased baking dish or cake pan, arranging them so they are touching.
12. Cover the pan with a clean kitchen towel or plastic wrap and let the Buchteln proof for an additional 30 minutes. They should puff up slightly.
13. Bake in the preheated oven for 20-25 minutes or until the Buchteln are golden brown and sound hollow when tapped on

the bottom.
Finish your Buchteln:
14. Remove the Buchteln from the oven and let them cool slightly.
15. Dust the Buchteln with powdered sugar for a delightful finish.

Austrian Pretzels

Servings: 8 pretzels
Preparation Time: 30 minutes
Resting Time: 1 hour 30 minutes
Baking Time: 12-15 minutes
Ingredients:
For the Pretzel Dough:
- 3 1/4 cups (400 grams) all-purpose flour
- 1 packet (2 1/4 teaspoons) active dry yeast
- 1 teaspoon salt
- 1 teaspoon granulated sugar
- 1 1/4 cups (300 milliliters) lukewarm water

For the Pretzel Bath:
- 8 cups (1.9 liters) water
- 1/2 cup (120 grams) baking soda

For Topping (optional):
- Coarse sea salt or pretzel salt

Instructions:
Prepare the Pretzel Dough:
1. In a small bowl, combine lukewarm water, active dry yeast, and granulated sugar. Stir gently and let it sit for about 5-10 minutes until it becomes frothy. This indicates that the yeast is active.
2. In a large mixing bowl, combine the all-purpose flour and salt.
3. Make a well in the center of the flour mixture and pour in the yeast mixture.
4. Gradually mix the ingredients together until a dough forms.
5. Turn the dough out onto a floured surface and knead it for about 8-10 minutes until it becomes smooth and elastic. You can add a little extra flour if it's too sticky, but try not to overdo it.
6. Place the dough in a greased bowl, cover it with a clean kitchen towel or plastic wrap, and let it rise in a warm, draft-free place for about 1 hour or until it has doubled in size.

Shape the Pretzels:
7. Once the dough has risen, gently punch it down to release any air

bubbles.
8. Divide the dough into 8 equal portions.
9. Roll each portion into a rope about 20-24 inches (50-60 centimeters) long.
10. Shape each rope into a pretzel by forming a U-shape. Cross the ends over each other, twist them once, and press them onto the curved part of the U to create the classic pretzel shape.

Prepare the Pretzel Bath:
11. Preheat your oven to 450°F (230°C). Line a baking sheet with parchment paper.
12. In a large, wide pot, bring 8 cups of water to a boil. Once boiling, add the baking soda carefully (it may bubble up) and stir until it dissolves.

Boil the Pretzels:
13. Carefully place each pretzel into the boiling water bath for about 30 seconds. Use a slotted spoon to flip them over halfway through.

Bake the Pretzels:
14. Remove the pretzels from the water bath and place them on the prepared baking sheet.
15. Optionally, sprinkle coarse sea salt or pretzel salt over the pretzels for a classic pretzel finish.
16. Bake in the preheated oven for 12-15 minutes or until the pretzels are golden brown and have a nice crust.

Cool and Enjoy:
17. Allow the pretzels to cool slightly before serving.
18. Serve your homemade Austrian pretzels warm with your favorite mustard or cheese dip.

Lebkuchen (Gingerbread Cookies)

Servings: Makes about 24 cookies
Preparation Time: 20 minutes
Chilling Time: 1 hour
Baking Time: 10-12 minutes
Ingredients:
For the Gingerbread Dough:
- 2 1/2 cups (300 grams) all-purpose flour
- 1 teaspoon baking powder
- 1/2 teaspoon baking soda

- 1/4 teaspoon salt
- 2 teaspoons ground ginger
- 2 teaspoons ground cinnamon
- 1/2 teaspoon ground cloves
- 1/2 teaspoon ground nutmeg
- 1/2 cup (115 grams) unsalted butter, softened
- 1/2 cup (100 grams) granulated sugar
- 1/2 cup (120 milliliters) molasses
- 1 large egg
- 1 teaspoon vanilla extract
- Zest of 1 orange (optional)

For the Icing (optional):

- 1 cup (120 grams) powdered sugar
- 2-3 tablespoons milk
- Food coloring (optional)

Instructions:

Prepare the Gingerbread Dough:

1. In a mixing bowl, whisk together the all-purpose flour, baking powder, baking soda, salt, and the ground spices (ginger, cinnamon, cloves, and nutmeg). Set this dry mixture aside.
2. In another large mixing bowl, cream together the softened unsalted butter and granulated sugar until the mixture is light and fluffy.
3. Add the molasses, egg, vanilla extract, and orange zest (if using) to the creamed butter and sugar. Mix until well combined.
4. Gradually add the dry flour mixture to the wet ingredients, mixing until a dough forms. The dough will be soft and slightly sticky.
5. Divide the dough into two equal portions and shape each portion into a disc.
6. Wrap each disc of dough in plastic wrap and refrigerate for at least 1 hour, or until the dough is firm and easy to handle.

Roll and Cut the Cookies:

7. Preheat your oven to 350°F (175°C). Line baking sheets with parchment paper.
8. Take one disc of dough out of the refrigerator at a time.
9. On a floured surface, roll out the dough to a thickness of about 1/4 inch (0.6 centimeters).
10. Use cookie cutters to cut out gingerbread shapes from the rolled

dough. Gather and reroll any scraps to make more cookies.
11. Place the cut-out cookies on the prepared baking sheets, leaving a little space between each one.

Bake the Lebkuchen:
12. Bake in the preheated oven for 10-12 minutes or until the edges of the cookies are slightly golden.
13. Remove the cookies from the oven and let them cool on the baking sheets for a few minutes before transferring them to a wire rack to cool completely.

Decorate the Cookies (Optional):
14. If desired, mix together powdered sugar and a few tablespoons of milk to create a simple icing. Add food coloring if you'd like to color the icing.
15. Use a piping bag or a small zip-top bag with a corner snipped off to pipe icing onto the cooled cookies in decorative patterns.

Vanillekipferl (Vanilla Crescent Cookies)

Servings: Makes about 24 cookies
Preparation Time: 20 minutes
Chilling Time: 30 minutes
Baking Time: 10-12 minutes
Ingredients:
For the Cookie Dough:
- 1 cup (225 grams) unsalted butter, softened
- 2/3 cup (80 grams) powdered sugar
- 1 3/4 cups (200 grams) all-purpose flour
- 1 1/4 cups (150 grams) ground almonds or hazelnuts
- 1 teaspoon vanilla extract
- A pinch of salt

For Rolling and Dusting:
- 1/2 cup (60 grams) powdered sugar
- 2 packets of vanilla sugar (or 2 teaspoons vanilla sugar)
- 1/2 cup (60 grams) finely chopped nuts (optional, for coating)

Instructions:
Prepare the Cookie Dough:
1. In a mixing bowl, cream together the softened unsalted butter and powdered sugar until the mixture is light and fluffy.
2. Add the vanilla extract and a pinch of salt to the butter-sugar mixture and mix until well combined.

3. Gradually add the all-purpose flour and ground almonds or hazelnuts to the mixture. Mix until a soft dough forms.
4. Divide the dough in half and shape each half into a flat disc.
5. Wrap each disc of dough in plastic wrap and refrigerate for about 30 minutes. Chilling the dough makes it easier to work with.

Shape the Vanillekipferl:

6. Preheat your oven to 350°F (175°C). Line baking sheets with parchment paper.
7. Remove one disc of dough from the refrigerator at a time.
8. Take small portions of the dough and roll them into ropes about 3/4 inch (2 centimeters) in diameter.
9. Cut the ropes into small pieces, about 2 inches (5 centimeters) long.
10. Shape each piece into a crescent shape by rolling it between your palms and then bending it slightly.
11. Place the shaped Vanillekipferl on the prepared baking sheets, leaving a little space between each one.

Bake the Cookies:

12. Bake in the preheated oven for 10-12 minutes or until the cookies are set but not yet browned.

Coat the Vanillekipferl:

13. While the cookies are still warm, carefully roll them in a mixture of powdered sugar and vanilla sugar until they are well coated. If desired, roll them in finely chopped nuts for added flavor and texture.

Marmor-Gugelhupf (Marble Cake)

Servings: 10-12 slices
Preparation Time: 20 minutes
Baking Time: 50-60 minutes
Ingredients:
For the Cake:
- 2 1/2 cups (300 grams) all-purpose flour
- 2 teaspoons baking powder
- 1/2 teaspoon salt
- 1 cup (225 grams) unsalted butter, softened
- 1 1/2 cups (300 grams) granulated sugar
- 4 large eggs
- 2 teaspoons vanilla extract

- 1/2 cup (120 milliliters) milk
- 2 tablespoons unsweetened cocoa powder

For the Chocolate Glaze (optional):
- 1/2 cup (90 grams) semisweet chocolate chips
- 2 tablespoons unsalted butter
- 1 tablespoon corn syrup (optional, for shine)

Instructions:

Prepare the Marble Cake:

1. Preheat your oven to 350°F (175°C). Grease and flour a Gugelhupf or Bundt cake pan, ensuring that it's well coated to prevent sticking.
2. In a mixing bowl, whisk together the all-purpose flour, baking powder, and salt. Set this dry mixture aside.
3. In another large mixing bowl, cream together the softened unsalted butter and granulated sugar until the mixture is light and fluffy.
4. Add the eggs one at a time, beating well after each addition. Stir in the vanilla extract.
5. Gradually add the dry flour mixture to the wet ingredients, alternating with the milk. Begin and end with the dry ingredients, mixing until just combined. Do not overmix.
6. Divide the cake batter in half into two separate bowls.

Prepare the Chocolate Batter:

7. In one of the bowls of cake batter, sift in the unsweetened cocoa powder. Mix until it's fully incorporated, creating the chocolate batter.

Layer and Swirl the Batter:

8. Spoon alternating dollops of the vanilla and chocolate batters into the prepared cake pan. Use a butter knife or a skewer to gently swirl the batters together to create a marbled effect. Be careful not to overmix; you want distinct swirls.

Bake the Marble Cake:

9. Place the cake pan in the preheated oven and bake for 50-60 minutes, or until a toothpick inserted into the center of the cake comes out clean or with a few moist crumbs.
10. Remove the cake from the oven and let it cool in the pan for about 10 minutes.
11. After 10 minutes, carefully invert the cake onto a wire rack to cool completely.

Prepare the Chocolate Glaze (optional):
12. In a microwave-safe bowl or a double boiler, melt the semisweet chocolate chips and unsalted butter together until smooth. Stir in the corn syrup if you'd like to add shine to the glaze.

Finish and Serve your Marmor-Gugelhupf:
13. Once the cake has cooled, drizzle the chocolate glaze over the top of the cake, allowing it to drizzle down the sides.
14. Allow the glaze to set for a few minutes.
15. Slice and serve your delicious Marmor-Gugelhupf, a delightful marble cake that combines the flavors of vanilla and chocolate in every bite. Enjoy with a cup of coffee or tea.

Bienenstich (Bee Sting Cake)

Servings: 10-12 slices
Preparation Time: 30 minutes
Baking Time: 25-30 minutes
Chilling Time: 2 hours (for the filling to set)
Ingredients:
For the Cake:
- 2 cups (250 grams) all-purpose flour
- 2 teaspoons baking powder
- 1/2 cup (115 grams) unsalted butter, softened
- 1/2 cup (100 grams) granulated sugar
- 2 large eggs
- 1 teaspoon vanilla extract
- 1/2 cup (120 milliliters) milk

For the Almond Topping:
- 1/2 cup (115 grams) unsalted butter
- 1/2 cup (100 grams) granulated sugar
- 2 tablespoons honey
- 2 cups (200 grams) sliced almonds

For the Filling:
- 1 1/2 cups (360 milliliters) heavy cream
- 2 tablespoons powdered sugar
- 1 teaspoon vanilla extract

Instructions:
Prepare the Cake:
1. Preheat your oven to 350°F (175°C). Grease and flour a 9x13-inch (23x33 cm) rectangular cake pan or a similar-sized baking

dish.
2. In a mixing bowl, whisk together the all-purpose flour and baking powder. Set this dry mixture aside.
3. In another large mixing bowl, cream together the softened unsalted butter and granulated sugar until the mixture is light and fluffy.
4. Add the eggs one at a time, beating well after each addition. Stir in the vanilla extract.
5. Gradually add the dry flour mixture to the wet ingredients, alternating with the milk. Begin and end with the dry ingredients, mixing until just combined. Do not overmix.
6. Spread the cake batter evenly in the prepared baking dish.

Prepare the Almond Topping:

7. In a saucepan, melt the unsalted butter, granulated sugar, and honey over medium heat. Bring the mixture to a gentle boil.
8. Stir in the sliced almonds and cook for about 2-3 minutes, or until the mixture thickens slightly and the almonds turn golden brown.
9. Pour the almond topping evenly over the cake batter in the baking dish.

Bake the Cake:

10. Place the baking dish in the preheated oven and bake for 25-30 minutes or until the cake is golden brown and a toothpick inserted into the center comes out clean.
11. Remove the cake from the oven and let it cool completely in the baking dish.

Prepare the Filling:

12. In a mixing bowl, whip the heavy cream, powdered sugar, and vanilla extract until stiff peaks form.

Assemble the Bienenstich:

13. Once the cake has cooled, carefully remove it from the baking dish.
14. Cut the cake in half horizontally to create two layers.
15. Spread the whipped cream filling evenly over the bottom layer of the cake.
16. Gently place the top layer of the cake over the filling.

Chill and Serve:

17. Refrigerate the assembled Bienenstich for at least 2 hours to allow the filling to set.

18. Slice and serve your delicious Bienenstich, a classic German and Austrian treat known for its honey and almond topping and creamy filling. Enjoy!

PRESERVES AND CONDIMENTS

Hausgemachte Senf (Homemade Mustard)

Ingredients:
- 1/2 cup (120 grams) yellow mustard seeds
- 1/2 cup (120 milliliters) white wine vinegar
- 1/4 cup (60 milliliters) water
- 2 tablespoons brown sugar
- 1 teaspoon salt
- 1/2 teaspoon ground turmeric
- 1/2 teaspoon ground paprika
- 1/4 teaspoon ground garlic (optional)
- 1/4 teaspoon ground chili powder (optional)

Instructions:
1. In a bowl, combine the yellow mustard seeds, white wine vinegar, and water. Mix well to ensure all the seeds are coated.
2. Cover the bowl with plastic wrap or a lid and let it sit at room temperature for 24 hours. This soaking process allows the mustard seeds to absorb the liquid and soften.
3. After 24 hours, the mustard seeds will have absorbed most of the liquid and will appear plump.
4. Transfer the soaked mustard seeds to a food processor or blender.
5. Add the brown sugar, salt, ground turmeric, ground paprika, and any optional spices you prefer, such as ground garlic or chili

powder.
6. Blend the mixture until it reaches your desired consistency. You can make it smooth or leave it slightly coarse for a grainier texture.
7. Taste the homemade mustard and adjust the seasoning if needed by adding more salt, sugar, or spices according to your preference.
8. Transfer the mustard to a clean glass jar or container with a tight-fitting lid.
9. Seal the container and refrigerate your homemade mustard. Allow it to sit in the refrigerator for at least 24 hours before using to allow the flavors to meld and mellow.
10. Your Hausgemachte Senf is now ready to enjoy as a condiment for sausages, sandwiches, and a wide range of Austrian dishes.

Storage:
- Homemade mustard can be stored in the refrigerator for several months in a tightly sealed container.

Variations:
- Experiment with different types of mustard seeds, such as brown or black, for unique flavors.
- Adjust the level of spiciness by adding more or less chili powder or ground black pepper.

Marillenmarmelade (Apricot Jam)

Ingredients:
- 2 pounds (about 900 grams) ripe apricots
- 2 cups (400 grams) granulated sugar
- Juice of 1 lemon
- 1 teaspoon lemon zest (optional)

Instructions:
1. Start by washing and drying the apricots. Remove the pits and cut the apricots into small pieces. You can leave the skin on for added texture and flavor.
2. Place the apricot pieces in a large, heavy-bottomed pot.
3. Add the granulated sugar and lemon juice to the pot with the apricots. If desired, you can also add lemon zest for extra citrusy aroma.
4. Stir the mixture well to combine all the ingredients.
5. Let the apricot mixture sit for about 30 minutes to allow the

sugar to dissolve and the apricots to release their juices.
6. After the resting period, place the pot over medium-high heat and bring the mixture to a boil, stirring frequently.
7. Once it's boiling, reduce the heat to a simmer and continue cooking the jam, stirring occasionally, for about 30-40 minutes or until it reaches the desired consistency. The jam should thicken and coat the back of a spoon.
8. To test the readiness of the jam, place a small amount on a chilled plate or spoon. Allow it to cool for a minute, then run your finger through it. If it wrinkles and holds its shape, it's ready.
9. Once the apricot jam is done, remove it from the heat and let it cool for a few minutes.
10. Carefully ladle the hot jam into sterilized jars, leaving about 1/4-inch (6 millimeters) of headspace at the top.
11. Seal the jars with airtight lids while the jam is still hot. This helps create a vacuum seal.
12. Allow the jars to cool completely at room temperature. As they cool, you may hear the lids pop, indicating a successful seal.
13. Store your homemade Marillenmarmelade in a cool, dark place. Once opened, keep it in the refrigerator.

Storage:
- Unopened jars of apricot jam can be stored in a cool, dark place for up to a year. Once opened, store in the refrigerator for several weeks.

Variations:
- Add a vanilla bean or a touch of almond extract for a different flavor dimension.
- For a chunkier jam, leave larger pieces of apricot in the mixture.

Eingelegte Gurken (Pickled Cucumbers)

Ingredients:
- 2 pounds (about 900 grams) small cucumbers (Kirby or pickling cucumbers work well)
- 2 cups (480 milliliters) water
- 2 cups (480 milliliters) white vinegar
- 1/4 cup (50 grams) granulated sugar
- 2 tablespoons salt
- 1 onion, thinly sliced
- 2 cloves garlic, peeled and sliced

- 1 teaspoon black peppercorns
- 1 teaspoon mustard seeds
- 1/2 teaspoon coriander seeds
- 1/2 teaspoon dill seeds (optional)
- Fresh dill sprigs (optional)
- Red pepper flakes (optional, for added heat)

Instructions:

1. Begin by washing the cucumbers thoroughly. Trim the ends, and if the cucumbers are large, you can slice them into spears or rounds. Leave smaller cucumbers whole.
2. In a large pot, combine the water, white vinegar, granulated sugar, and salt. Stir well to dissolve the sugar and salt.
3. Add the thinly sliced onion, garlic slices, black peppercorns, mustard seeds, coriander seeds, and any optional spices you prefer, such as dill seeds or red pepper flakes. These spices will infuse the pickling liquid with flavor.
4. Bring the mixture to a boil over medium-high heat. Once it's boiling, reduce the heat and let it simmer for about 5 minutes. This allows the flavors to meld and the pickling liquid to become aromatic.
5. While the pickling liquid simmers, pack the prepared cucumbers into clean, sterilized glass jars. You can add fresh dill sprigs between the cucumbers for extra flavor and visual appeal.
6. Carefully ladle the hot pickling liquid into the jars, covering the cucumbers and spices. Leave about 1/2 inch (1.25 centimeters) of headspace at the top of each jar.
7. Seal the jars with sterilized, airtight lids while the pickles and liquid are still hot. This helps create a proper seal.
8. Allow the jars to cool to room temperature before storing them in a cool, dark place.
9. Let the pickles sit for at least one week to develop their flavor. The longer they sit, the more pronounced their taste will become.
10. Once opened, store the jars in the refrigerator for several weeks.

Storage:

- Unopened jars of pickled cucumbers can be stored in a cool, dark place for up to a year. Once opened, store in the refrigerator for several weeks.

Variations:

- Customize the pickles by adding sliced peppers, carrots, or other

vegetables for a colorful mix.
- Experiment with different spices and herbs to create unique flavor profiles.

Kren (Horseradish Sauce)

Ingredients:
- 1/2 cup (120 grams) fresh horseradish root, peeled and grated
- 1/4 cup (60 milliliters) white wine vinegar
- 1/4 cup (60 milliliters) water
- 2 tablespoons granulated sugar
- 1/2 teaspoon salt
- 1/2 teaspoon freshly ground black pepper
- 1/2 cup (120 milliliters) heavy cream

Instructions:
1. Begin by peeling the fresh horseradish root and grating it using a fine grater. Be cautious as horseradish can be quite pungent, so grate it in a well-ventilated area.
2. In a saucepan, combine the grated horseradish, white wine vinegar, water, granulated sugar, salt, and freshly ground black pepper.
3. Place the saucepan over medium heat and bring the mixture to a simmer. Stir well to dissolve the sugar and salt.
4. Once it's simmering, reduce the heat to low and let it cook for about 5-7 minutes. This will mellow the sharpness of the horseradish.
5. Remove the saucepan from the heat and let the horseradish mixture cool to room temperature.
6. In a separate bowl, whip the heavy cream until it forms stiff peaks.
7. Once the horseradish mixture has cooled, gently fold in the whipped cream until well combined.
8. Transfer your homemade Kren to a clean glass jar or container with a tight-fitting lid.
9. Seal the container and refrigerate the horseradish sauce. It will be ready to use once it has chilled for a few hours.
10. Serve Kren as a condiment alongside roasted meats, sausages, or Wiener Schnitzel. It adds a zesty and creamy element to your Austrian dishes.

Storage:

- Homemade horseradish sauce can be stored in the refrigerator for up to a week.

Variations:
- Adjust the intensity of the horseradish by using more or less grated horseradish root.
- You can add a squeeze of lemon juice or a dash of white wine for a different flavor twist.

Apfelkompott (Apple Compote)

Ingredients:
- 4-5 medium-sized apples (e.g., Granny Smith, Gala, or Fuji)
- 1/4 cup (50 grams) granulated sugar (adjust to taste)
- 1/2 cup (120 milliliters) water
- 1 cinnamon stick
- 2-3 cloves
- 1/2 teaspoon vanilla extract (optional)

Instructions:
1. Start by peeling, coring, and slicing the apples into bite-sized pieces.
2. In a saucepan, combine the apple slices, granulated sugar, water, cinnamon stick, and cloves.
3. Place the saucepan over medium heat and bring the mixture to a gentle simmer.
4. Once it's simmering, reduce the heat to low and let the apples cook, stirring occasionally, for about 10-15 minutes or until they become tender and start to break down.
5. If using vanilla extract, stir it into the compote during the last few minutes of cooking.
6. Taste the apple compote and adjust the sweetness by adding more sugar if desired.
7. Remove the saucepan from the heat and let the compote cool slightly. The compote will thicken as it cools.
8. You can serve the apple compote warm, at room temperature, or chilled, depending on your preference.
9. Enjoy your homemade Apfelkompott on its own as a comforting dessert, or use it as a topping for pancakes, waffles, ice cream, or as a filling for pastries and crepes.

Storage:
- Store any leftover apple compote in an airtight container in the

refrigerator for up to a week.

Variations:
- Experiment with different apple varieties to create unique flavor profiles.
- Add a squeeze of lemon juice for a touch of brightness.

Rote Rüben Kren (Beetroot Horseradish)

Ingredients:
- 2 medium-sized beetroots, cooked and peeled
- 1/2 cup (120 grams) fresh horseradish root, peeled and grated
- 1/4 cup (60 milliliters) white wine vinegar
- 1/4 cup (60 milliliters) water
- 2 tablespoons granulated sugar
- 1/2 teaspoon salt
- 1/2 teaspoon freshly ground black pepper
- 1/2 teaspoon lemon zest (optional)

Instructions:
1. Begin by cooking the beetroots. You can boil them until tender, roast them in the oven, or use pre-cooked beets. Once cooked, let them cool and then peel and dice them into small pieces.
2. Grate the fresh horseradish root using a fine grater. Be cautious as horseradish can be pungent, so grate it in a well-ventilated area.
3. In a saucepan, combine the diced beetroots, grated horseradish, white wine vinegar, water, granulated sugar, salt, freshly ground black pepper, and lemon zest if using.
4. Place the saucepan over medium heat and bring the mixture to a simmer. Stir well to dissolve the sugar and salt.
5. Once it's simmering, reduce the heat to low and let it cook for about 5-7 minutes. This will mellow the sharpness of the horseradish and allow the flavors to meld.
6. Remove the saucepan from the heat and let the mixture cool to room temperature.
7. Transfer your homemade Rote Rüben Kren to a clean glass jar or container with a tight-fitting lid.
8. Seal the container and refrigerate the beetroot horseradish. It will be ready to use once it has chilled for a few hours.
9. Serve Rote Rüben Kren as a condiment alongside cold cuts, sandwiches, and traditional Austrian dishes. It adds a colorful and zesty twist to your meals.

Storage:
- Homemade beetroot horseradish can be stored in the refrigerator for up to a week.

Variations:
- Adjust the balance of sweetness and heat by adding more or less horseradish or sugar.
- Experiment with different spices and herbs for unique flavor combinations.

Preiselbeeren (Cranberry Sauce)

Ingredients:
- 12 ounces (340 grams) fresh cranberries
- 1 cup (200 grams) granulated sugar (adjust to taste)
- 1 cup (240 milliliters) water
- Zest and juice of 1 orange (optional)
- 1 cinnamon stick (optional)
- 1/4 teaspoon ground cloves (optional)

Instructions:
1. Start by rinsing the fresh cranberries thoroughly under cold water and removing any stems or damaged berries.
2. In a saucepan, combine the cranberries, granulated sugar, and water.
3. If desired, add the zest and juice of 1 orange for a citrusy twist.
4. You can also add a cinnamon stick and ground cloves for extra flavor depth.
5. Place the saucepan over medium-high heat and bring the mixture to a boil.
6. Once it's boiling, reduce the heat to low and let it simmer, stirring occasionally, for about 10-15 minutes or until the cranberries have burst and the sauce has thickened.
7. Taste the cranberry sauce and adjust the sweetness by adding more sugar if desired.
8. Remove the saucepan from the heat and let the sauce cool to room temperature. As it cools, it will continue to thicken.
9. Once the cranberry sauce has cooled, transfer it to a clean glass jar or container.
10. Seal the container and refrigerate the cranberry sauce. It will be ready to use once it has chilled for a few hours.
11. Serve Preiselbeeren alongside roast meats, sausages, or festive

dishes. Its sweet-tart flavor complements a variety of Austrian and holiday meals.

Storage:
- Homemade cranberry sauce can be stored in the refrigerator for up to a week.

Variations:
- Add a splash of red wine or port for a richer flavor.
- Experiment with different spices like star anise or nutmeg for unique twists.

Tomatenketchup (Tomato Ketchup)

Ingredients:
- 2 pounds (about 900 grams) ripe tomatoes, roughly chopped
- 1 onion, finely chopped
- 2 cloves garlic, minced
- 1/2 cup (120 milliliters) white vinegar
- 1/4 cup (50 grams) granulated sugar
- 1 teaspoon salt
- 1/2 teaspoon ground black pepper
- 1/2 teaspoon paprika
- 1/4 teaspoon ground cloves
- 1/4 teaspoon ground allspice
- 1/4 teaspoon ground cinnamon

Instructions:
1. Begin by placing the roughly chopped tomatoes in a large saucepan. Cook them over medium heat, stirring occasionally, until they start to break down and release their juices. This will take about 15-20 minutes.
2. Use a potato masher or an immersion blender to puree the cooked tomatoes until smooth.
3. In the same saucepan, add the finely chopped onion and minced garlic. Continue to cook over medium heat, stirring occasionally, until the onions become translucent, about 5 minutes.
4. Stir in the white vinegar, granulated sugar, salt, ground black pepper, paprika, ground cloves, ground allspice, and ground cinnamon.
5. Reduce the heat to low and let the mixture simmer, uncovered, for about 45-60 minutes. Stir occasionally to prevent sticking and promote even cooking.

6. As the ketchup cooks, it will gradually thicken and reduce. You'll know it's ready when it reaches your desired consistency.
7. Taste the tomato ketchup and adjust the sweetness, saltiness, or spice level to your liking by adding more sugar, salt, or spices.
8. Remove the saucepan from the heat and let the tomato ketchup cool to room temperature.
9. Once it has cooled, transfer the homemade Tomatenketchup to clean glass bottles or jars with tight-fitting lids.
10. Seal the containers and refrigerate the ketchup. It will be ready to use once it has chilled for a few hours.
11. Enjoy your homemade tomato ketchup as a condiment for burgers, hot dogs, fries, or as a dipping sauce for a variety of dishes.

Storage:
- Homemade tomato ketchup can be stored in the refrigerator for up to a month.

Variations:
- Experiment with different spices or add a dash of hot sauce for a spicy ketchup.
- For a smoky twist, include a pinch of smoked paprika.

Hollersirup (Elderflower Syrup)

Ingredients:
- 20-25 elderflower heads, freshly picked and free from insects
- 4 cups (1 liter) water
- 4 cups (800 grams) granulated sugar
- 1 organic lemon, sliced
- 1 organic orange, sliced (optional)
- 1-2 tablespoons citric acid (optional, for preservation)

Instructions:
1. Begin by gently shaking the elderflower heads to remove any insects or debris. Do not rinse the flowers, as they will lose some of their flavor.
2. In a large pot, combine the water and granulated sugar. Stir well to dissolve the sugar.
3. Add the elderflower heads to the pot, followed by the slices of lemon and orange, if using.
4. If you want to extend the shelf life of the syrup, you can add citric acid at this point.

5. Place the pot over medium-high heat and bring the mixture to a boil. Once it's boiling, reduce the heat to low and let it simmer gently for about 10 minutes.
6. Remove the pot from the heat and let the elderflower syrup cool to room temperature. The syrup will become more fragrant as it cools.
7. Once the syrup has cooled, strain it through a fine-mesh sieve or cheesecloth into clean, sterilized bottles or jars. Discard the spent elderflower heads and citrus slices.
8. Seal the bottles or jars with airtight lids and store the elderflower syrup in the refrigerator.
9. Your Hollersirup is now ready to use. To make a refreshing elderflower drink, simply mix a few tablespoons of syrup with sparkling or still water, and enjoy.

Storage:
- Homemade elderflower syrup can be stored in the refrigerator for several months. If you added citric acid, it will have a longer shelf life.

Variations:
- You can add a few sprigs of fresh mint or a slice of fresh ginger to the syrup for unique flavor profiles.
- For a floral twist, try adding a few lavender buds during the simmering process.

Made in the USA
Las Vegas, NV
03 October 2023